RAVE REVIE...

POSITIO...

☆   ☆   ☆

ALSO BY AL RIES AND JACK TROUT

Marketing Warfare

POSITIONING

THE BATTLE FOR YOUR MIND

Al Ries and Jack Trout

WARNER BOOKS

A Time Warner Company

WARNER BOOKS EDITION

Copyright © 1981, 1986 by McGraw-Hill Inc.
All rights reserved. Except as permitted under the United States Copyright Act of 1976, no part of this publication may be reproduced or distributed in any form or by any means, or stored in a data base or retrieval system, without the prior written permission of the publisher.

Cover design by Diane Luger
Cover illustration by Jeff Nishinaka

This Warner Books Edition is published by arrangement with McGraw-Hill Book Company, 1221 Avenue of the Americas, New York, N.Y. 10020

Warner Books, Inc.
1271 Avenue of the Americas
New York. N.Y. 10020

Visit our Web site at
http://warnerbooks.com

 A Time Warner Company

Printed in the United States of America

First Warner Books Printing: March, 1982

First Warner Books Revised Edition Printing: October, 1986

Reissued: February, 1993

20   19   18

Dedicated to the second best
advertising agency in the whole world.

Whoever they might be.

Contents

Introduction

"Positioning" is the first body of thought to come to grips with the problems of communicating in an overcommunicated society. . .1

Chapter 1. What Positioning Is All About

Many people misunderstand the role of communication in business and politics today. In our overcommunicated society, very little communication actually takes place. Rather, a company must create a "position" in the prospect's mind. A position that takes into consideration not only a company's own strengths and weaknesses, but those of its competitors as well.................5

Chapter 2. The Assault on the Mind

There are just too many companies, too many products, too much marketing noise. The per-capita consumption of advertising in America is $376 per year. 11

Chapter 3. Getting Into the Mind

The easy way to get into a person's mind is to be first. If you can't be first, then you must find a way to position yourself against the product, the politician, the person who did get there first.....19

Chapter 4. Those Little Ladders in Your Head

To cope with our overcommunicated society, people have learned to rank products on mental ladders. In the rent-a-car field, for example, most people put Hertz on the top rung, Avis on the second rung, and National on the third. Before you can position anything, you must know where it is on the product ladder in the mind. 29

Chapter 5. You Can't Get There from Here
A competitor has no hope of going head-to-head against the position IBM has established in computers. Many companies have ignored this basic positioning principle and have suffered the consequences. 37

Chapter 6. Positioning of a Leader
To be a leader you have to be first to get into the mind of the prospect—and then follow the strategies for staying there. . . . 43

Chapter 7. Positioning of a Follower
What works for a leader doesn't necessarily work for a follower. An also-ran must find a "creneau" or hole in the mind not occupied by someone else. 53

Chapter 8. Repositioning the Competition
If there are no "creneaus" left, you have to create one by repositioning the competition. Tylenol, for example, repositioned aspirin. 61

Chapter 9. The Power of the Name
The most important marketing decision you can make is what to name the product. The name alone has enormous power in an overcommunicated society. 71

Chapter 10. The No-Name Trap
Companies with long, complex names have tried to shorten them by using initials. This strategy seldom works. 85

Chapter 11. The Free-Ride Trap
Can a second product get a free ride on the advertising coattails of a well-known brand? In the case of products like LifeSavers gum, the answer is no. 95

Chapter 12. The Line-Extension Trap
Line extension has become the marketing sickness of the past decade. Why it seldom works. 101

Chapter 13. When Line Extension Can Work
There are cases, however, of successful line extension (GE, for example.) A discussion of when to use the house name and when to use a new name. 115

Chapter 14. Positioning a Company: Xerox
Xerox owns the copier position. But as Xerox moves into the office automation field, how should the company be positioned? . .127

Chapter 15. Positioning a Country: Belgium
The answer to the problems of a national airline like Sabena Belgium World Airlines is to position the country, not the airline. 137

Chapter 16. Positioning an Island: Jamaica
"Sand and surf" has become a visual cliché for all Caribbean islands. How do you establish a unique position for one of them? 143

Chapter 17. Positioning a Product: Milk Duds
How a product with a small budget can get into the mind by positioning itself as the long-lasting alternative to the candy bar. .149

Chapter 18. Positioning a Service: Mailgram
Why a totally new service has to be positioned against the old. 153

Chapter 19. Positioning a Long Island Bank
How a bank successfully struck back when its territory was invaded by its giant neighbors from the Big City. 159

Chapter 20. Positioning a New Jersey Bank
One of the best ways to establish a position is to find a weakness in your competitor's. 167

Chapter 21. Positioning a ski resort: Stowe
How an outside expert can add credibility to a positioning claim. 173

Chapter 22. Positioning the Catholic Church
Even institutions can benefit from positioning thinking. An outline

of the logical steps that could be taken to position the Roman Catholic Church. 177

Chapter 23. Positioning Yourself and Your Career
You can benefit by using positioning strategy to advance your own career. Key principle: Don't try to do everything yourself. Find a horse to ride 183

Chapter 24. Positioning Your Business
To get started on a positioning program, there are six questions you can ask yourself. 193

Chapter 25. Playing the Positioning Game
To be successful at positioning, you have to have the right mental attitude. You have to become an outside-in thinker rather than an inside-out thinker. This requires patience, courage, and strength of character. 201

Index 211

Introduction

"What we have here is a failure to communicate."

How often have you heard that bromide? "Failure to communicate" is the single, most common, most universal reason people give for their problems.

Business problems, government problems, labor problems, marriage problems.

If only people took the time to communicate their feelings, to explain their reasons, the assumption is that many of the problems of the world would somehow disappear. People seem to believe any problem can be solved if only the parties sit down and talk.

Unlikely.

Today, communication itself is the problem. We have become the world's first overcommunicated society. Each year, we send more and receive less.

A new approach to communication

This book has been written about a new approach to communication called *positioning*. And most of the examples are from the most difficult of all forms of communication—advertising. A form of communication that, from the point of view of the recipient, is held in low esteem. Advertising is, for the most part, unwanted and unliked. In some cases, advertising is thoroughly detested.

To many intellectuals, advertising is selling your soul to corporate America—a subject not worthy of serious study.

In spite of its reputation, or perhaps because of it, the field of advertising is a superb testing ground for theories of communication. If it works in advertising, most likely it will work in politics, religion, or any other activity that requires mass communication.

So the examples in this book could just as well have been taken from the field of politics, war, business, or even the science of chasing the opposite sex. Or any form of human activity which involves influencing the minds of other people. Whether you want to promote a car, a cola, a computer, a candidate, or your own career.

Positioning is a concept that has changed the nature of advertising, a concept so simple, people have difficulty understanding how powerful it is.

Every successful politician practices positioning. So do Procter & Gamble and Johnson & Johnson.

Positioning defined

Positioning starts with a product. A piece of merchandise, a service, a company, an institution, or even a person. Perhaps yourself.

But positioning is not what you do to a product. Positioning is what you do to the mind of the prospect. That is, you position the product in the mind of the prospect.

So it's incorrect to call the concept "product positioning." You're not really doing something to the product itself.

Not that positioning doesn't involve change. It often does. But changes made in the name, the price, and the package are really not changes in the product at all. They're basically cosmetic changes done for the purpose of securing a worthwhile position in the prospect's mind.

Positioning is the first body of thought that comes to grips with the difficult problem of getting heard in our overcommunicated society.

How positioning got started

If one word can be said to have marked the course of advertising in the past decade, the word is "positioning."

Positioning has become a buzzword among advertising, sales, and marketing people. Not only in America, but around the world. Teachers, politicians, and editorial writers are using the word.

Most people think positioning got started in 1972 when we wrote a series of articles entitled "The Positioning Era" for the trade paper *Advertising Age*.

Since then, we have given more than 1000 speeches on positioning to advertising groups in 21 different countries around the world. And we have given away more than 150,000 copies of our "little orange booklet" which reprints the *Advertising Age* articles.

Positioning has changed the way the advertising game is being played today.

"We're the third largest-selling coffee in America," say the Sanka radio commercials.

The third largest? Whatever happened to those good old advertising words like "first" and "best" and "finest"?

Well, the good old advertising days are gone forever and so are the words. Today you find comparatives, not superlatives.

"Avis is only No. 2 in rent-a-cars, so why go with us? We try harder."

"Seven-Up: the uncola."

Along Madison Avenue, these are called positioning slogans. And the advertising people who write them spend their time and research money looking for positions, or holes, in the marketplace.

But positioning has stirred up interest well beyond Madison Avenue. With good reason.

Anyone can use positioning strategy to get ahead in the game of life. And look at it this way: If you don't understand and use the principles, your competitors undoubtedly will.

1 What positioning is all about

How did a hard-sell concept like positioning become so popular in a business noted for its creativity?

In truth, the past decade might well be characterized as a "return to reality." White knights and black eye patches gave way to such positioning concepts as "Lite Beer from Miller. Everything you always wanted in a beer. And less."

Poetic? Yes. Artful? Yes. But also a straightforward, clearly defined explanation of the basic positioning premise.

To be successful today, you must touch base with reality. And the only reality that counts is what's already in the prospect's mind.

To be creative, to create something that doesn't already exist in the mind, is becoming more and more difficult. If not impossible.

The basic approach of positioning is not to create something new and different, but to manipulate what's already up there in the mind, to retie the connections that already exist.

Today's marketplace is no longer responsive to the strategies that worked in the past. There are just too many products, too many companies, and too much marketing noise.

The question most frequently asked by positioning skeptics is, "Why?" Why do we need a new approach to advertising and marketing?

The overcommunicated society

The answer is that we have become an overcommunicated society. The per-capita consumption of advertising in America today is $376.62 a year. (That compares with $16.87 in the rest of the world.)

If you spend $1 million a year on advertising, you are bombarding the average consumer with less than a half cent of advertising, spread out over 365 days—a consumer already exposed to $376.61½ worth of other advertising.

In our overcommunicated society, to talk about the "impact" of your advertising is to seriously overstate the potential effectiveness of your message. Advertising is not a sledgehammer. It's more like a light fog, a very light fog that envelops your prospects.

In the communication jungle out there, the only hope to score big is to be selective, to concentrate on narrow targets, to practice segmentation. In a word, "positioning."

The mind, as a defense against the volume of today's communications, screens and rejects much of the information offered it. In general, the mind accepts only that which matches prior knowledge or experience.

Millions of dollars have been wasted trying to change minds with advertising. Once a mind is made up, it's almost impossible to change it. Certainly not with a weak force like advertising. "Don't confuse me with the facts, my mind's made up." That's a way of life for most people.

The average person will sit still when being told something which he or she knows nothing about. (Which is why "news" is an effective advertising approach.) But the average person cannot tolerate being told he or she is wrong. Mind-changing is the road to advertising disaster.

The oversimplified mind

The only defense a person has in our overcommunicated society is an oversimplified mind.

Not unless they repeal the law of nature that gives us only 24 hours in a day will they find a way to stuff more into the mind.

The average mind is already a dripping sponge that can only soak up more information at the expense of what's already there. Yet we continue to pour more information into that supersaturated sponge and are disappointed when our messages fail to get through.

Advertising, of course, is only the tip of the communication iceberg. We communicate with each other in a wide variety of bewildering ways. And in a geometrically increasing volume.

The medium may not be the message, but it does seriously affect the message. Instead of a transmission system, the medium acts like a filter. Only a tiny fraction of the original material ends up in the mind of the receiver.

Furthermore, what we receive is influenced by the nature of our overcommunicated society. "Glittering generalities" have become a way of life in our overcommunicated society. We oversimplify because that's the only way to cope.

Technically, we are capable of increasing the volume of communication at least tenfold. We're experimenting with direct television broadcasting from satellites. Every home would have 100 channels or so to choose from.

North American Philips has just introduced a 3½-inch compact disc that holds 600 megabytes of data, more than enough to store the entire *Encyclopaedia Britannica*.

Terrific. But who is working on a compact disc for the mind? Who is trying to help the prospect cope with complexity that so overwhelms the mind that the average reaction to the wealth of information today is to tighten the intake valve? To accept less and less of what is so freely available? Communication itself is the communication problem.

The oversimplified message

The best approach to take in our overcommunicated society is the oversimplified message.

In communication, as in architecture, less is more. You have to sharpen your message to cut into the mind. You have to jettison the ambiguities, simplify the message, and then simplify it some more if you want to make a long-lasting impression.

People who depend on communication for their livelihood know the necessity of oversimplification.

Let's say you are meeting with a politician whom you are trying to get elected. In the first 5 minutes, you'll learn more about your political product than the average voter is going to learn about that person in the next 5 years.

Since so little material about your candidate is ever going to get into the mind of the voter, your job is really not a "communication" project in the ordinary meaning of the word.

It's a selection project. You have to select the material that has the best chance of getting through.

The enemy that is keeping your messages from hitting pay dirt is the volume of communication. Only when you appreciate the nature of the problem can you understand the solution.

When you want to communicate the advantages of a political candidate or a product or even yourself, you must turn things inside out.

You look for the solution to your problem not inside the product, not even inside your own mind.

You look for the solution to your problem inside the prospect's mind.

In other words, since so little of your message is going to get through anyway, you ignore the sending side and concentrate on the receiving end. You concentrate on the perceptions of the prospect. Not the reality of the product.

"In politics," said John Lindsay, "the perception is the reality." So, too, in advertising, in business, and in life.

But what about truth? What about the facts of the situation?

What is truth? What is objective reality? Every human being seems to believe intuitively that he or she alone holds the key to universal truth. When we talk about truth, what truth are we talking about? The view from the inside or the view from the outside?

It does make a difference. In the words of another era, "The customer is always right." And by extension, the seller or communicator is always wrong.

It may be cynical to accept the premise that the sender is wrong and the receiver is right. But you really have no other choice. Not if you want to get your message accepted by another human mind.

Besides, who's to say that the view from the inside looking out is any more accurate than the view from the outside looking in?

By turning the process around, by focusing on the prospect rather than the product, you simplify the selection process. You also learn principles and concepts that can greatly increase your communication effectiveness.

2 The assault on the mind

As a nation we have fallen in love with the concept of "communication." (In some grade schools "show and tell" is now being called "communication.") We don't always appreciate the damage being done by our overcommunicated society.

In communication, more is less. Our extravagant use of communication to solve a host of business and social problems has so jammed our channels that only a tiny fraction of all messages actually gets through. And not necessarily the most important ones either.

The transmission traffic jam

Take advertising, for example. With only 6 percent of the world's population, America consumes 57 percent of the world's advertising. (And you thought our use of energy was extravagant. Actually, we consume only 33 percent of the world's energy.)

Advertising, of course, is only a small channel in the communication river.

Take books. Each year some 30,000 books are published in America. Every year another 30,000. Which doesn't sound like a lot until you realize it would take 17 years of reading 24 hours a day just to finish one year's output.

Who can keep up?

Take newspapers. Each year American newspapers use more than 10 million tons of newsprint. Which means that the average person consumes 94 pounds of newsprint a year.

There's some question whether the average person can digest all this information. The Sunday edition of a large metropolitan newspaper like *The New York Times* weighs about 4½ pounds and contains some 500,000 words. To read it all, at an average reading speed of 300 words per minute, would take almost 28 hours. Not only would your Sunday be shot, but also a good part of the rest of the week too.

How much is getting through?

Take television. A medium barely 35 years old. A powerful and pervasive medium, television didn't replace radio or newspapers or magazines. Each of the three older media is bigger and stronger than it ever was.

Television is an additive medium. And the amount of communication added by television is awesome.

Ninety-eight percent of all American homes have at least one television set. (A third have two or more.)

Ninety-six percent of all television households can receive four or more TV stations. (A third can receive ten or more.)

The average American family watches television more than 7 hours a day. (More than 51 hours a week.)

Like motion pictures, the TV picture is really a still picture which changes 30 times a second. Which means the average American family is exposed to some 750,000 television pictures a day.

Not only are we being pictured to death, we are being papered to death. Take that Xerox machine down the hall. American business processes 1.4 trillion pieces of paper a year. That's 5.6 billion every working day.

Down the halls at the Pentagon, copy machines crank out 350,000 pages a day for distribution throughout the Defense Department. Equal to 1000 good-sized novels.

"World War II will end," said Field Marshal Montgomery, "when the warring nations run out of paper."

Take packaging. An 8-ounce package of Total breakfast cereal contains 1268 words of copy on the box. Plus an offer for a free booklet on nutrition. (Which contains another 3200 words.)

The assault on the mind takes place in many different ways. The U.S. Congress passes some 500 laws a year (that's bad enough), but regulatory agencies promulgate some 10,000 new rules and regulations in the same amount of time.

And the regulatory agencies are not stingy with their words either. Consider this: The Lord's Prayer contains 56 words; the Gettysburg Address, 266; the Ten Commandments, 297; the Declaration of Independence, 300; and a recent U.S. government order setting the price of cabbage, 26,911.

At the state level, over 250,000 bills are introduced each year. And 25,000 pass the legislatures to disappear into the labyrinths of the law.

Ignorance of the law is no excuse. Ignorance of the lawmakers apparently is. Our legislators continue to pass thousands of laws that you can't possibly keep track of. And even if you could, you couldn't possibly remember how a law might differ from one of our 50 states to another.

Who reads, sees, or listens to all this outpouring of communication?

There's a traffic jam on the turnpikes of the mind. Engines are overheating. Tempers are rising.

George Bush, Ted Kennedy, and Chevrolet

How much do you know about George Bush? Most people know just three things: (1) He's good-looking. (2) He's from Texas. (3) He's Vice President of the United States.

Not much for a person who's been in public service for a good part of his adult life. Yet that might be just enough to make Mr. Bush President of the United States in 1988.

Actually there are many people who don't know Mr. Bush as well as you might think. A *People* magazine poll showed that

44 percent of supermarket shoppers didn't know who George Bush was, even though he had been Vice President for 4 years.

On the other hand, 93 percent of the consumers recognized Mr. Clean, the genie on the bottle of the Procter & Gamble cleaner of the same name. They recognized Mr. Clean, even though he hadn't been seen on television in 10 years, which shows the power of advertising to register a simple message.

What do you know about Ted Kennedy? Probably a lot more than you know about George Bush. And probably enough to keep him from being the next President of the United States.

At best, communication in an overcommunicated society is difficult. Yet you are often better off if communication doesn't take place. At least until you are ready to position yourself for the long term. You never get a second chance to make a first impression.

What do the following names mean to you: Camaro, Cavalier, Celebrity, Chevette, Citation, Corvette, and Monte Carlo?

Automobile model names, right? Would you be surprised to learn that these are all Chevrolet models?

Chevrolet is one of the most heavily advertised products in the world. In a recent year, General Motors spent more than $178 million to promote Chevrolet in the United States. That's $487,000 a day, $20,000 an hour.

What do you know about Chevrolet? About Chevrolet engines, transmissions, tires? About the seats, upholstery, steering?

Be honest. How many Chevrolet models are you familiar with? And do you know the differences between them? Confusing, isn't it?

The only answer to the problems of an overcommunicated society is the positioning answer. To cut through the traffic jam in the prospect's mind, you must use Madison Avenue techniques.

Nearly half the jobs in the United States can be classified as information occupations. More and more people are trying to cope with the problems of our overcommunicated society.

Whether you have an information job or not, you can benefit from learning the lessons of Madison Avenue. At home and in the office.

The media explosion

Another reason our messages keep getting lost is the number of media we have invented to serve our communication needs.

There is television. Commercial, cable, and pay.

There's radio. AM and FM.

There's outdoor. Posters and billboards.

There are newspapers. Morning, evening, daily, weekly, and Sunday.

There are magazines. Mass magazines, class magazines, enthusiast magazines, business magazines, trade magazines.

And, of course, buses, trucks, streetcars, subways, and taxicabs. Generally speaking, anything that moves today is carrying a "message from our sponsor."

Even the human body has become a walking billboard for Adidas, Gucci, Benetton, and Gloria Vanderbilt.

Take advertising again. Just after World War II, the per-capita consumption of advertising in the United States was about $25 a year. Today it's 15 times as much. (Inflation accounts for part of this increase, but volume is also up substantially.)

Do you know 15 times as much about the products you buy? You may be exposed to much more advertising, but your mind can't absorb any more than it used to. There's a finite limit to how much you can take in, and advertising, even at $25 a year, was already way over the limit. That 1-quart container that sits on top of your neck can hold just so much.

At $376 per person, the average American consumer is already exposed to twice as much advertising per year as the average Canadian. Four times as much as the average English person. And five times as much as the average French person.

While no one doubts the advertiser's financial ability to dish it out, there's some question about the consumer's mental ability to take it all in.

Each day, thousands of advertising messages compete for a share of the prospect's mind. And make no mistake about it, the mind is the battleground. Between 6 inches of gray matter is where the advertising war takes place. And the battle is rough, with no holds barred and no quarter given.

Advertising is a brutal business where mistakes can be costly. But out of the advertising wars, principles have been developed to help you cope with our overcommunicated society.

The product explosion

Another reason our messages keep getting lost is the number of products we have invented to take care of our physical and mental needs.

Take food for example. The average supermarket in the United States has some 12,000 individual products or brands on display. For the consumer, there's no relief in sight. In fact, the product explosion could get worse. In Europe they are building super-supermarkets (called hypermarkets) with room for several times as many products. Biggs in Cincinnati, the first hypermarket in America, stocks 60,000 products.

The packaged-goods industry obviously expects the proliferation to continue. Those scratch marks on the side of most grocery boxes, the Universal Product Code, represent 10 digits. (Your social security number has only 9. And the system is designed to handle more than 200 million people.)

And this same situation holds in the industrial field. The Thomas Register, for example, lists 80,000 companies. There are 292 manufacturers of centrifugal pumps, 326 builders of electronic controls, to take two categories at random.

There are half a million active trademarks registered at the U.S. Patent Office. And 25,000 new ones get added every year. (Hundreds of thousands of products are sold without trademarks too.)

In a typical year, the 1500 companies listed on the New York Stock Exchange introduce more than 5000 "significant" new products. And presumably a lot more than that were insignificant. Not to mention the millions of products and services marketed by America's 5 million other corporations.

Take drugs. There are some 100,000 prescription drugs on the U.S. market. While many of these are specialized and used almost exclusively by medical specialists, the general practitioner still has a herculean job to keep informed about the multitude of drug products available.

Herculean? No, it's an impossible job. Even Hercules himself could not have kept up with more than a small fraction of these drugs. To expect more is to be totally ignorant of the finite capacity of even the most brilliant mind.

And how does the average person cope with the product and media explosions? Not very well. Studies on the sensitivity of the human brain have established the existence of a phenomenon called "sensory overload."

Scientists have discovered that a person is capable of receiving only a limited amount of sensation. Beyond a certain point, the brain goes blank and refuses to function normally. (Dentists have been toying with some of these discoveries. Earphones are placed on the patient, and the sound level is turned up until the sensation of pain no longer is felt.)

The advertising explosion

Ironically, as the effectiveness of advertising goes down, the use of it goes up. Not just in volume, but in the number of users.

Doctors, lawyers, dentists, accountants are dipping their toes into the advertising pool. Even institutions like churches, hospitals, and government have begun to advertise. (In a recent year the U.S. government spent $228,857,200 on advertising.)

Professional people used to consider advertising beneath their dignity. But as competition heats up, lawyers, dentists, optometrists, accountants, and architects are starting to promote themselves.

Cleveland-based Hyatt Legal Services is spending $4.5 million a year on television advertising. Jacoby & Meyers is another big legal advertiser.

Advertising is likely to start soon in the medical profession for a simple reason: Our overcommunicated society is in the process of becoming an overmedicated one too. A study for the Department of Health and Human Services predicts a surplus of about 70,000 doctors by 1990.

How will these excess doctors find patients to practice on? By advertising, of course.

But the professionals who are opposed to advertising say it downgrades their profession. And it does. To advertise effectively today, you have to get off your pedestal and put your ear to the ground. You have to get on the same wavelength as the prospect.

3

Getting into the mind

In our overcommunicated society, the paradox is that nothing is more important than communication. With communication going for you, anything is possible. Without it, nothing is possible. No matter how talented and ambitious you may be.

What's called luck is usually an outgrowth of successful communication. Saying the right things to the right person at the right time. Finding what the NASA people in Houston call a window in space.

Positioning is an organized system for finding a window in the mind. It is based on the concept that communication can only take place at the right time and under the right circumstances.

The easy way into the mind

The easy way to get into a person's mind is to be first. You can demonstrate the validity of this principle by asking yourself a few simple questions.

What's the name of the first person to fly solo across the North Atlantic? Charles Lindbergh, right?

Now, what's the name of the second person to fly solo across the North Atlantic?

Not so easy to answer, is it?

What's the name of the first person to walk on the moon? Neil Armstrong, of course.

What's the name of the second?

What's the name of the highest mountain in the world? Mount Everest in the Himalayas, right?

What's the name of the second highest mountain in the world?

What's the name of the first person you ever made love with?

What's the name of the second?

The first person, the first mountain, the first company to occupy the position in the mind is going to be awfully hard to dislodge.

Kodak in photography, Kleenex in tissue, Xerox in plain-paper copiers, Hertz in rent-a-cars, Coca in cola, General in electric.

The first thing you need to "fix your message indelibly in the mind" is not a message at all. It's a mind. An innocent mind. A mind that has not been burnished by someone else's brand.

What's true in business is true in nature too.

"Imprinting" is the term animal biologists use to describe the first encounter between a newborn animal and its natural mother. It takes only a few seconds to fix indelibly in the memory of the young animal the identity of its parent.

You might think all ducks look alike, but even a day-old duckling will always recognize its mother, no matter how much you mix up the flock.

Well, that's not quite true. If the imprinting process is interrupted by the substitution of a dog or cat or even a human being, the duckling will treat the substitute as its natural mother. No matter how different the creature looks.

Falling in love is a similar phenomenon. While people are more selective than ducks, they're not nearly as selective as you might think.

What counts most is receptivity. Two people must meet in a situation in which both are receptive to the idea. Both must have open windows. That is, neither is deeply in love with someone else.

Marriage, as a human institution, depends on the concept of first being better than best. And so does business.

If you want to be successful in love or in business, you must appreciate the importance of getting into the mind first.

You build brand loyalty in a supermarket the same way you build mate loyalty in a marriage. You get there first and then be careful not to give them a reason to switch.

The hard way into the mind

And what if your name is not Charles or Neil or Kleenex or Hertz? What if someone else got into your prospect's mind first?

The hard way to get into a person's mind is second. Second is nowhere.

What's the largest-selling book ever published? (Also the first book ever printed with movable type?) The Bible, of course.

And the second largest-selling book ever published? Who knows?

New York is the largest cargo port in the United States. But which one is second? Would you believe Hampton Roads, Virginia? It's true.

Who was the second person to fly solo across the North Atlantic? (Amelia Earhart was not the second person to fly the North Atlantic solo, although she was the first woman to do it. Now then, who was the second woman?)

If you didn't get into the mind of your prospect first (personally, politically, or corporately), then you have a positioning problem.

In a physical contest, the odds favor the fastest horse, the strongest team, the best player. "The race isn't always to the swift, nor the battle to the strong," said Damon Runyan, "but that's the way to bet."

Not so in a mental contest. In a mental battle the odds favor the first person, the first product, the first politician to get into the mind of the prospect.

In advertising, the first product to establish the position has an enormous advantage. Xerox, Polaroid, Bubble Yum, to name a few more examples.

In advertising, it's best to have the best product in your particular field. But it's even better to be first.

Love might be wonderful the second time around, but nobody cares who the second person to fly solo across the North Atlantic was. Even if that person was a better pilot.

There are positioning strategies to deal with the problem of being No. 2 or No. 3 or even No. 203. (See Chapter 8, "Repositioning the competition.")

But first make sure you can't find something to be first in. It's better to be a big fish in a small pond (and then increase the size of the pond) than to be a small fish in a big pond.

Advertising learns the lesson

The advertising industry is learning the Lindbergh lesson the hard way.

With the magic of money and enough bright people, some companies feel that any marketing program should succeed.

The wreckage is still washing up on the beach. DuPont's Corfam, Gablinger's beer, the Convair 880, Vote toothpaste, Handy Andy cleaner.

The world will never be the same again, and neither will the advertising business.

Not that a lot of companies haven't tried. Every drugstore and supermarket is filled with shelf after shelf of "half successful" brands. The manufacturers of these me-too products cling to the hope that they can develop a brilliant advertising campaign which will lift their offspring into the winner's circle.

Meanwhile, they hang in there with coupons, deals, point-of-purchase displays. But profits are hard to come by, and that "brilliant" advertising campaign, even if it comes, doesn't ever seem to turn the brand around. No wonder management people turn skeptical when the subject of advertising comes up.

It's enough to drive an advertising person into the soft ice cream business.

The chaos in the marketplace is a reflection of the fact that advertising just doesn't work the way it used to. But old traditional ways of doing things die hard. "There's no reason why advertising can't do the job," say the defenders of the status quo, "as long as the product is good, the plan is sound, and the commercials are creative."

But they overlook one big, loud reason. The marketplace itself. The noise level today is far too high.

Messages prepared in the old, traditional ways have no hope of being successful in today's overcommunicated society.

To understand how we got to where we are today, it might be helpful to take a quick look at recent communication history.

The product era

Back in the fifties, advertising was in the product era. In a lot of ways, these were the good old days when the "better mousetrap" and some money to promote it were all you needed.

It was a time when advertising people focused their attention on product features and customer benefits. They looked for, as Rosser Reeves called it, the "Unique Selling Proposition."

But in the late fifties, technology started to rear its ugly head. It became more and more difficult to establish that "USP."

The end of the product era came with an avalanche of me-too products that descended on the market. Your "better mousetrap" was quickly followed by two more just like it. Both claiming to be better than the first one.

Competition was fierce and not always honest. It got so bad that one product manager was overheard to say, "Wouldn't you know it. Last year we had nothing to say, so we put 'new and improved' on the package. This year the research people came up with a real improvement, and we don't know what to say."

The image era

The next phase was the image era. Successful companies found that reputation, or image, was more important in selling a product than any specific product feature.

The architect of the image era was David Ogilvy. As he said in his famous speech on the subject, "Every advertisement is a long-term investment in the image of a brand." And he proved the validity of his ideas with programs for Hathaway shirts, Rolls-Royce, Schweppes, and others.

But just as the me-too products killed the product era, the me-too companies killed the image era. As every company tried to establish a reputation for itself, the noise level became so high that relatively few companies succeeded.

And of the ones that made it, most did it primarily with spectacular technical achievements, not spectacular advertising. Xerox and Polaroid, to name two.

The positioning era

Today it has become obvious that advertising is entering a new era—an era where creativity is no longer the key to success.

The fun and games of the sixties and seventies have given way to the harsh realities of the eighties.

To succeed in our overcommunicated society, a company must create a position in the prospect's mind, a position that takes into consideration not only a company's own strengths and weaknesses, but those of its competitors as well.

Advertising is entering an era where strategy is king. In the positioning era, it's not enough to invent or discover something. It may not even be necessary. You must, however, be first to get into the prospect's mind.

IBM didn't invent the computer. Sperry-Rand did. But IBM was the first company to build a computer position in the mind of the prospect.

What Amerigo discovered

The Sperry-Rand of the fifteenth century was Christopher Columbus.

As every schoolchild knows, the man who discovered America was poorly rewarded for his efforts. Christopher Columbus made the mistake of looking for gold and keeping his mouth shut.

Amerigo Vespucci didn't. The IBM of the fifteenth century, Amerigo was 5 years behind Christopher. But he did two things right.

First, he positioned the New World as a separate continent, totally distinct from Asia. This caused a revolution in the geography of his day.

Second, he wrote extensively of his discoveries and theories. Especially significant are the five letters of his third voyage. One (Mundus Novus) was translated into 40 different languages over a 25-year period.

Before he died, Spain granted him Castilian citizenship and gave him a major state post.

As a result, the Europeans credited Amerigo Vespucci with the discovery of America and named the place after him.

Christopher Columbus died in jail.

What Michelob discovered

The great copywriters of yesterday, who have gone to the big ad agency in the sky, would die all over again if they saw some of the campaigns currently running.

Take beer advertising, for example. In the past a beer copywriter looked closely at the product to find a copy platform. And he or she found product features like "real-draft" Piels and "cold-brewed" Ballantine.

And even further back a beer copywriter searched for just the right words to paint a picture of quality, taste, and appetite appeal.

"Just a kiss of the hops."

"From the land of sky blue waters."

Today, however, poetry in advertising is as dead as poetry in poetry.

One of the biggest advertising successes of recent times is the campaign for Michelob. The brand was launched with a campaign that is as poetic as a stop sign. And just as effective.

"First class is Michelob" positioned the brand as a premium-priced American-made beer. In a few years, Michelob became one of the largest-selling beers in the United States. At premium prices too.

Was Michelob the first premium-priced domestic beer? No, of course not. But Michelob was the first to build the position in the beer-drinker's mind.

What Miller discovered

Notice how the poetry in the old Schlitz beer slogan hides the positioning.

"Real gusto in a great, light beer."

Did anyone out there in the neighborhood bar and grill believe that Schlitz was any lighter than Budweiser or Pabst? No, the Schlitz slogan made as much sense to the Joe Sixpacks of this world as the lyrics in an Italian opera.

But over at the Miller Brewing Company, they apparently asked themselves what would happen if they really positioned a beer as a light beer.

So Miller introduced "Lite" beer. And the rest is history. A runaway success that spawned a host of me-too brands. Including, ironically, Schlitz Light. (Presumably to be promoted as: "Real gusto in a great, light, light beer.")

For many people or products today, one roadway to success is to look at what your competitors are doing and then subtract the poetry or creativity which has become a barrier to getting the message into the mind. With a purified and simplified message, you can then penetrate the prospect's mind.

For example, there's an imported beer whose positioning strategy is so crystal-clear that those old-time beer copywriters probably wouldn't even accept it as advertising.

"You've tasted the German beer that's the most popular in America. Now taste the German beer that's the most popular in Germany." This is how Beck's beer effectively positioned itself against Lowenbrau.

Advertising like this made Beck's beer popular in America too. Sales kept going up year after year. Lowenbrau, on the other hand, gave up the struggle and became a domestic brand.

Strange things have been happening in American advertising. It's becoming less poetic—and more effective.

4 Those little ladders in your head

To better understand what your message is up against, let's take a closer look at the ultimate objective of all communication: the human mind.

Like the memory bank of a computer, the mind has a slot or position for each bit of information it has chosen to retain. In operation, the mind is a lot like a computer.

But there is one important difference. A computer has to accept what you put into it. The mind does not. In fact, it's quite the opposite.

The mind rejects new information that doesn't "compute." It accepts only that new information which matches its current state of mind. It filters out everything else.

You see what you expect to see

Take any two abstract drawings. Write the name Schwartz on one and the name Picasso on the other. Then ask someone for an opinion. You see what you expect to see.

Ask two people of opposite persuasion, say, a Democrat and a Republican, to read an article on a controversial subject. Then ask each one if the article changed his or her opinion.

You'll find that the Democrat gets out of the article facts to support one point of view. The Republican gets out of the same article facts to support the opposite point of view. Very little mind changing takes place. You see what you expect to see.

Pour a bottle of Gallo into an empty 50-year-old bottle of French Burgundy. Then carefully decant a glass in front of a friend and ask for an opinion.

You taste what you expect to taste.

Blind taste testings of champagne have often ranked inexpensive California brands above French ones. With the labels on, this is unlikely to happen.

You taste what you expect to taste.

Were it not so, there would be no role for advertising at all. Were the average consumer rational instead of emotional, there would be no advertising. At least not as we know it today.

One prime objective of all advertising is to heighten expectations. To create the illusion that the product or service will perform the miracles you expect. And presto, that's exactly what the advertising does.

But create the opposite expectation and the product is in trouble. The introductory advertising for Gablinger's beer created a feeling that because it was a diet product, it would taste bad.

And sure enough, the advertising worked! People tried it and were easily convinced that it did taste bad. You taste what you expect to taste.

An inadequate container

Not only does the human mind reject information which does not match its prior knowledge or experience, it doesn't have much prior knowledge or experience to work with.

In our overcommunicated society, the human mind is a totally inadequate container.

According to Harvard psychologist Dr. George A. Miller, the average human mind cannot deal with more than seven units at a time. Which is why seven is a popular number for lists that have to be remembered. Seven-digit phone numbers, the

Seven Wonders of the World, seven-card stud, Snow White and the Seven Dwarfs.

Ask someone to name all the brands he or she remembers in a given product category. Rarely will anyone name more than seven. And that's for a high-interest category. For low-interest products, the average consumer can usually name no more than one or two brands.

Try listing all ten of the Ten Commandments. If that's too difficult, how about the seven danger signals of cancer? Or the four horsemen of the Apocalypse?

In one newspaper survey, 80 out of 100 Americans couldn't name a single member of the President's Cabinet.

If our mental storage bowl is too small to handle questions like these, how in the world are we going to keep track in our mind of all those brand names which have been multiplying like rabbits over the years?

Thirty years ago the six leading cigarette companies between them offered the American smoker 17 different brands. Today they sell more than 175. (A vending machine built to hold all these brands would have to be 30 feet long.)

"Modelitus" has struck every industry, from automobiles to beer to zoom lenses. Detroit currently sells 290 different models in a bewildering variety of styles and sizes. Caravelle, Capri, Cimarron, Camaro, Calais, Cutlass. Let's see, is it a Chevrolet Caravelle or a Plymouth Caravelle? The public is confused.

To cope with complexity, people have learned to simplify everything.

When asked to describe an offspring's intellectual progress, a person doesn't usually quote vocabulary statistics, reading comprehension, mathematical ability, etc. "He's in seventh grade" is a typical reply.

This ranking of people, objects, and brands is not only a convenient method of organizing things but also an absolute necessity to keep from being overwhelmed by the complexities of life.

The product ladder

To cope with the product explosion, people have learned to rank products and brands in the mind. Perhaps this can best be visualized by imagining a series of ladders in the mind. On each step is a brand name. And each different ladder represents a different product category.

Some ladders have many steps. (Seven is many.) Others have few, if any.

A competitor that wants to increase its share of the business must either dislodge the brand above (a task that is usually impossible) or somehow relate its brand to the other company's position.

Yet too many companies embark on marketing and advertising programs as if the competitor's position did not exist. They advertise their products in a vacuum and are disappointed when their messages fail to get through.

Moving up the ladder in the mind can be extremely difficult if the brands above have a strong foothold and no leverage or positioning strategy is applied.

An advertiser who wants to introduce a new product category must carry in a new ladder. This, too, is difficult, especially if the new category is not positioned against the old one. The mind has no room for what's new and different unless it's related to the old.

That's why if you have a truly new product, it's often better to tell the prospect what the product is not, rather than what it is.

The first automobile, for example, was called a "horseless" carriage, a name which allowed the public to position the concept against the existing mode of transportation.

Words like "off-track" betting, "lead-free" gasoline, and "sugar-free" soda are all examples of how new concepts can best be positioned against the old.

The "against" position

In today's marketplace the competitor's position is just as important as your own. Sometimes more important. An early success in the positioning era was the famous Avis campaign.

The Avis campaign will go down in marketing history as a classic example of establishing the "against" position. In the case of Avis, this was a position against the leader.

"Avis is only No. 2 in rent-a-cars, so why go with us? We try harder."

For 13 years in a row, Avis lost money. Then they admitted that they were No. 2 and Avis started to make money.

The first year Avis made $1.2 million. The second year, $2.6 million. The third year, $5 million. Then the company was sold to ITT.

Avis was able to make substantial gains because they recognized the position of Hertz and didn't try to attack them head-on.

To better understand why the Avis program was so successful, let's look into the mind of the prospect and imagine we can see a product ladder marked "rent-a-cars."

On each rung of the product ladder is a brand name. Hertz on top. Avis on the second rung. National on the third.

Many marketing people have misread the Avis story. They assume the company was successful because it tried harder.

Not at all. Avis was successful because it related itself to Hertz. (If trying harder were the secret of success, Harold Stassen would have been President many times over.)

As an indication of how far the advertising business has come in its acceptance of comparative ads, *Time* magazine originally rejected the "We try harder" line as being too competitive with Hertz. Other magazines followed the *Time* lead.

So the account executive panicked and agreed to change the line to "We try damned hard." (A curse word presumably being less offensive than a comparative word.)

Only after the ad was canceled did *Time* change its mind and agree to accept the original version. (The account executive was fired.)

Establishing the "against" position is a classic positioning maneuver. If a company isn't the first, then it has to be the first to occupy the No. 2 position. It's not an easy task.

But it can be done. What Avis is doing in rent-a-cars, Burger King is doing in fast foods, and Pepsi is doing in colas.

The "uncola" position

Another classic positioning strategy is to worm your way onto a ladder owned by someone else. As 7-Up did. The brilliance of this idea can only be appreciated when you comprehend the enormous share of mind enjoyed by Coke and Pepsi. Almost two out of every three soft drinks consumed in the United States are cola drinks.

By linking the product to what was already in the mind of the prospect, the "uncola" position established 7-Up as an alternative to a cola drink. (The three rungs on the cola ladder might be visualized as: One, Coke. Two, Pepsi, And three, 7-Up.)

To prove the universality of positioning concepts, McCormick Communications took beautiful-music radio station WLKW, an also-ran in the Providence (Rhode Island) market, and made it number one. Their theme: WLKW, the unrock station.

To find a unique position, you must ignore conventional logic. Conventional logic says you find your concept inside yourself or inside the product.

Not true. What you must do is look inside the prospect's mind.

You won't find an "uncola" idea inside a 7-Up can. You find it inside the cola drinker's head.

The F.W.M.T.S. trap

More than anything else, successful positioning requires consistency. You must keep at it year after year.

Yet after a company has executed a brilliant positioning coup, too often it falls into what we call the F.W.M.T.S. trap: "Forgot what made them successful."

Shortly after the company was sold to ITT, Avis decided it was no longer satisfied with being No. 2. So it ran ads saying, "Avis is going to be No. 1."

That's advertising your aspirations. Wrong psychologically. And wrong strategically.

Avis was not destined to be No. 1 unless it could find a weakness in Hertz to exploit.

Furthermore, the old campaign not only related No. 2 Avis to No. 1 Hertz on the product ladder in the prospect's mind, but also capitalized on the natural sympathy people have for the underdog.

The new campaign was just conventional brag-and-boast advertising.

Be honest. In the last 20 years, Avis has run many different advertising campaigns: "The wizard of Avis." "You don't have to run through airports."

But what is the single theme that leaps into your mind when someone mentions Avis?

Of course, "Avis is only No. 2, etc." Yet Avis in the last few years has consistently ignored the only concept it really owns in the mind. Someday when National Rent-A-Car passes Avis in sales, Avis will appreciate the value of the No. 2 concept it lost.

If you want to be successful today, you can't ignore the competitor's position. Nor can you walk away from your own. In the immortal words of Joan Didion, "Play it as it lays."

5

You can't get there from here

There's an old story about a traveler who asked a farmer for directions to a nearby town.

The farmer replied, "Well, you go down the road for a mile, turn left at the fork. No, that won't work."

"You turn around and drive for half a mile till you hit a stop sign, then turn right," the farmer continued. "No, that won't work either." After a long pause, the farmer looked at the confused traveler and said, "You know what, son, you can't get there from here!"

That just happens to be the fate of many people, politicians, and products today. They happen to be in a position where "they can't get there from here."

Avis is not going to be No. 1. Wishing won't make it so. And neither will massive amounts of advertising.

The "can do" spirit refuses to die

In many ways our country's Vietnam experience was a typical example of American "can do" spirit. Anything is possible if only you try hard enough. But no matter how hard we tried, no matter how many soldiers and how much money we poured in, the problem could not be solved by an outside force.

We couldn't get there from here.

In spite of hundreds of Vietnam examples to the contrary, we live in a "can do" environment. Yet many things are not possible, no matter how hard you try.

Take the 55-year-old executive vice president who is never going to get the top job. When the chief executive retires in a few years at age 65, the board appoints a 48-year-old successor.

The 55-year-old is out of phase for the president's job. To have a chance for promotion, he or she must be at least a decade younger than the current holder.

In the battle for the mind, the same thing often happens to the product that's out of phase.

Today a company can have a great product, a great sales force, a great advertising campaign and still fail miserably if it happens to be in a position in which "you can't get there from here." No matter how many millions it is prepared to spend.

And the best example is what happened to RCA in the computer business.

The handwriting on the wall

In 1969 we wrote an article for *Industrial Marketing* magazine using RCA as one of the prime examples. Entitled "Positioning Is a Game People Play in Today's Me-Too Marketplace," the article pulled no punches. It named names and made predictions, all based on the rules of a game called positioning. (It was the first time anyone had used the word "positioning" to describe the process of coping with the mental position that a larger, more established competitor occupies.)

One prediction, in particular, turned out to be strikingly accurate. As far as the computer industry was concerned, we wrote, "A company has no hope to make progress head-on against the position that IBM has established."

The operative word, of course, was "head-on." And while it's possible to compete successfully with a market leader (the article suggested several approaches), the rules of positioning say it can't be done "head-on."

Back in 1969 this raised a few eyebrows. Who were we to say that a powerful, multibillion-dollar company like RCA couldn't find happiness in the computer business if it so desired?

So as 1970 rolled around, it was full speed ahead at RCA. The incredible story was told in the pages of the business press.

"RCA fires a broadside at No. 1," said the headline of an article in the September 19, 1970, issue of *Business Week*.

"RCA goes head-to-head with IBM," said the headline of a news item in the October 1970 issue of *Fortune*.

"RCA computer push is head-on slash at IBM," said the headline of a story in the October 26, 1970, issue of *Advertising Age*.

And just to make sure there was no mistaking the company's intentions, Robert W. Sarnoff, chairman and president, made a prediction that by the end of 1970, RCA would be in a "firm No. 2 position" in the computer industry. Pointing out that his company had already invested "far more to develop a strong position in the computer industry than we have ever put into any previous business venture," including color TV, Mr. Sarnoff said that the goal had been development of a solid profit position in the early seventies.

The "can do" spirit dies

Less than a year later, the roof fell in. "The $250 million disaster that hit RCA," said the headline of a story in the September 25, 1971, issue of *Business Week*.

That's a lot of dough. Someone figured out that if you took that much money in one-hundred-dollar bills and put it on the sidewalk in Rockefeller Center, the stack would go right past Bob Sarnoff's window on the 53rd floor of the RCA Building.

Those were bad times for computer manufacturers. In May 1970, after years of unprofitable computer operations, General Electric threw in the sponge by selling the mess to Honeywell.

With two major computer manufacturers folding one right after another, the urge to say "I told you so" was irresistible.

So later in the year 1971, we came back with "Positioning Revisited: Why Didn't GE and RCA Listen?" (The article appeared in the November 1971 issue of *Industrial Marketing*.)

How do you advertise and market against a company like IBM? The two positioning articles made some suggestions.

How to go against an IBM

The computer business has often been referred to as "Snow White and the Seven Dwarfs." Snow White has established a position unrivaled in the history of marketing.

IBM has 70 percent of the mainframe computer business vs. less than 10 percent for the largest of the dwarfs.

How do you go against a company with a position like IBM?

Well, first you have to recognize it. Then you don't do the thing that too many people in the computer field try to do. Act like IBM.

A company has no hope to make progress head-on against the position that IBM has established. And history, so far, has proved this to be true.

The small companies in the field probably recognize this. But the big companies seem to think they can take their strong positions against IBM. Well, as one unhappy executive was heard to say, "There just isn't enough money in the world." You can't get there from here.

"Fight fire with fire" is the old cliché. But as the late Howard Gossage used to say, "That's silly. You fight fire with water."

A better strategy for IBM's competitors would be to take advantage of whatever positions they already own in the minds of their prospects and then relate them to a new position in computers. For example, how should RCA have positioned its computer line?

Our 1969 article made a suggestion: "RCA is a leader in communications. If they positioned a computer line that related to their business in communications, they could take advantage of their own position. Even though they would be ignoring a great deal of business, they would be establishing a strong beachhead."

Take General Electric, a company that is a big user of computers. Time sharing was the big technological topic of the day. If GE had concentrated on time-sharing computers, they too might have succeeded in the computer field. (Actually, the only computer operation General Electric didn't sell to Honeywell was their time-sharing network, which remains profitable to this day.)

Take NCR, a company with a strong position in cash registers.

NCR has made great progress in the computer business by concentrating its efforts on retail data entry systems. Computerized cash registers, if you will.

Where the situation is hopeless, however, the effort in finding a valid position is probably wasted. Much better to concentrate on other areas of a company's business. As Charlie Brown said, "No problem is too big to run away from."

In truth, outright failure is often preferable to mediocre success.

An also-ran can easily be tempted to think that the answer to the problem is trying harder. A company stuck with a losing position is not going to benefit much from hard work.

The problem is not what, but when, The extra effort, if it is going to be of much help, should be applied early to establish the precious posture of product leadership.

With it, everything is possible. Without it, the going is going to be rough indeed. (As the Eskimo remarked, the lead dog is the only one who enjoys a change of view.)

Smith and Jones at General Electric

One example might help illustrate the principle. Two gentlemen had their eyes on the top job at General Electric. One was named Smith. The other was named Jones.

Smith was your typical "can do" corporate executive. So when he was given the computer operation to run, he accepted the assignment with relish.

Jones, on the other hand, was realistic. He knew that GE hadn't gotten into the computer business early enough to dominate it. At this late stage of the game, it was going to cost the company too much to catch up to IBM. If it ever could.

After Smith failed to turn the computer business around, Jones got a chance to participate. He recommended that General Electric get out of the computer business, which it eventually did by selling the operation to Honeywell.

That's one reason why Reginald H. Jones wound up as chief executive of the General Electric Company. And J. Stanford Smith wound up at International Paper.

In a nutshell, the hierarchy in the computer business is duplicated in almost every other industry. Invariably, every industry has a strong leader (IBM in computers, Xerox in copiers, and General Motors in automobiles) and a host of also-rans.

If one can understand the role of positioning in the computer industry, then one can transfer this knowledge to almost any other situation.

What works for computers will also work for cars and for colas.

Or vice versa.

6 Positioning of a leader

Companies like Avis and Seven-Up found viable alternative positions to marketing leaders.

But most companies don't want to be an also-ran, successful or not. They want to be a leader like Hertz or Coke.

So how do you get to be the leader? Actually it's quite simple. Remember Charles Lindbergh and Neil Armstrong?

You just get there firstest with the mostest.

Establishing leadership

History shows that the first brand into the brain, on the average, gets twice the long-term market share of the No. 2 brand and twice again as much as the No. 3 brand. And the relationships are not easily changed.

The leader brand in category after category outsells the number two brand by a wide margin. Hertz outsells Avis, General Motors outsells Ford, Goodyear outsells Firestone, McDonald's outsells Burger King, General Electric outsells Westinghouse.

Many marketing experts overlook the enormous advantages of being first. Too often they attribute successes like Kodak and IBM and Coke to "marketing acumen."

The failures of leaders

Yet when the shoe is on the other foot, when a marketing leader isn't first in a new category, the new product is usually an also-ran.

Coca-Cola is a gigantic company compared with Dr. Pepper. Yet when Coke introduced a competitive product, Mr. Pibb, even the immense resources of the Atlanta giant couldn't put much of a dent in Dr. Pepper's sales. Mr. Pibb remains a poor second.

IBM is a much bigger company than Xerox and has awesome resources of technology, work force, and money. Yet what happened when IBM introduced a line of copiers competitive with those of Xerox?

Not much. Xerox still has a share of the copier market several times that of IBM.

And supposedly Kodak was going to cream Polaroid when the Rochester colossus got into the instant camera business. Far from it. Kodak managed to take only a small share, at the expense of a substantial loss in its conventional camera business.

Almost all the advantages accrue to the leader. In the absence of any strong reasons to the contrary, consumers will probably select the same brand for their next purchase as they selected for their last purchase. Stores are more likely to stock the leading brands.

The larger, more successful companies usually have the first pick of outstanding college graduates. In fact, they usually attract more and better employees.

At almost every step of the way, the leading brand has the advantage.

On an airplane flight, for example, the airline will often stock one brand of cola, one brand of ginger ale, one brand of beer, etc.

On your next flight, see if the three brands aren't Coke, Canada Dry, and Budweiser, the three leading brands of cola, ginger ale, and beer.

The instability of equality

It's true that in some categories the two leading brands run neck and neck.

What's equally true is that these categories are inherently unstable. Sooner or later, you can expect one brand to get the upper hand and open a lead which eventually will reach a stable 5 to 3 or 2 to 1 ratio.

Consumers are like chickens. They are much more comfortable with a pecking order that everybody knows about and accepts.

Hertz and Avis.

Harvard and Yale.

McDonald's and Burger King.

When two brands are close, one or the other is likely to get the upper hand and then dominate the market for years to come.

Between 1925 and 1930, for example, Ford and Chevrolet were locked in a head-to-head battle. Then Chevrolet took the lead in 1931.

In the model years since, including dislocations caused by depression and wars, Chevrolet has lost the lead only four times to Ford.

The time for extra effort is clearly when the situation is in doubt. When neither side has a clearcut superiority. Winning the battle for sales leadership in a single year will often clinch the victory for decades to come.

It takes 110 percent of rated power for a jet to get its wheels off the ground. Yet when it reaches 30,000 feet, the pilot can throttle back to 70 percent of power and still cruise at 600 miles per hour.

Strategies for maintaining leadership

Question: Where does the 800-pound gorilla sleep? Answer: Anywhere he wants to.

Leaders can do anything they want to. Short-term, leaders are almost invulnerable. Momentum alone carries them along.

(Old wrestling expression: You can't get pinned when you're on top.)

For General Motors, Procter & Gamble, and the leaders of this world, the worries are never about this year or next. Their worries are long-term. What's going to happen 5 years from now? 10 years from now?

Leaders should use their short-term flexibility to assure themselves of a stable long-term future. As a matter of fact, the marketing leader is usually the one who moves the ladder into the mind with his or her brand nailed to the one and only rung. Once there, what should leaders do and not do?

What not to do

As long as a company owns the position, there's no point in running advertisements that repeat the obvious. "We're No. 1" is a typical example.

Much better is to enhance the product category in the prospect's mind. IBM's advertising usually ignores competition and sells the value of computers. All computers, not just the company's types.

Why isn't it a good idea to run advertising that says, "We're No. 1"?

The reason is psychological. Either the prospect knows you are No. 1 and wonders why you are so insecure that you have to say so. Or the prospect doesn't know you are No. 1. If not, why not?

Maybe you have defined your leadership in your own terms and not the prospect's terms. Unfortunately, that just won't work.

You can't build a leadership position on your own terms. "The best-selling under-$1000 high-fidelity system east of the Mississippi."

You have to build a leadership position in the prospect's terms.

What to do

"The real thing." This classic Coca-Cola advertising campaign is a strategy that can work for any leader.

The essential ingredient in securing the leadership position is getting into the mind first. The essential ingredient in keeping that position is reinforcing the original concept. Coca-Cola is the standard by which all others are judged. In contrast, everything else is an imitation of "the real thing."

This is not the same as saying "We're No. 1." The largest brand could be the largest seller because it has a lower price, it is available in more outlets, etc.

But "the real thing," like a first love, will always occupy a special place in the prospect's mind.

"We invented the product." A powerful motivating force behind Xerox copiers. Polaroid cameras. Zippo lighters.

Covering all bets

Unfortunately, leaders often read their own advertising so avidly they end up thinking they can do no wrong. So when a competitor introduces a new product or a new feature, the tendency is to pooh-pooh the development.

Leaders should do the opposite. They should cover all bets. This means a leader should swallow his or her pride and adopt every new product development as soon as it shows signs of promise.

General Motors spent $50 million to cover the Wankel engine when it was offered to the automotive industry. Money down the drain? Not necessarily.

General Motors probably looks on the $50 million spent to buy a Wankel license as cheap insurance to protect an $84 billion-a-year business.

Suppose the Wankel had become the automotive engine of the future. And Ford or Chrysler had been the first to buy the rights. Where would General Motors be now?

Right where Kodak and 3M are in office copiers. When these two leaders in coated-paper copiers had a chance to cover by buying rights to Carlson's xerography process, they declined.

"Nobody would pay 5 cents for a plain-paper copy when they could get a coated-paper copy for a cent and a half." Logical enough. But the essence of covering is protection against the unexpected.

And the unexpected did happen. Haloid took a chance on the Carlson patents, and today the company (successively Haloid Xerox and then Xerox) is a $9 billion giant. Bigger than 3M and only a step behind Kodak. *Fortune* calls the Xerox 914 plain-paper copier "probably the single most profitable product ever manufactured in the United States."

And what did Xerox do for an encore?

Almost nothing. The spectacular success of the 914 was followed by one failure after another. Most notably in computers.

Power from the product

"Only when our office copying success has been repeated, not once, but several times," said the Xerox chairman early on in the company's diversification game, "can we fairly reach the conclusion that this organization has the kind of power that can be relied upon again and again."

This is the classic mistake made by the leader. The illusion that the power of the product is derived from the power of the organization.

It's just the reverse. The power of the organization is derived from the power of the product, the position that the product owns in the prospect's mind.

Coca-Cola has power. The Coca-Cola Company is merely a reflection of that power.

Outside the cola field, the Coca-Cola Company has to earn its power the hard way—either by getting into the mind first, by establishing a strong alternative position, or by repositioning the leader.

So Coca-Cola's Mr. Pibb runs a poor second to Dr. Pepper, and all the power of the Coca-Cola Company can't do much about it.

So, too, with Xerox. The power is in the position that Xerox owns in the mind. Xerox means copier. Xerox owns the copier position because it got into the mind first and then exploited that copier position by a massive marketing program.

But in computers, office duplicators, word processors, and other products, Xerox starts at ground zero. Xerox has obviously tried to duplicate its copier success in other fields. But it has apparently forgotten one essential element of the 914 program. It was the first to fly the plain-paper copier ocean.

Covering with multibrands

Most leaders should cover competitive moves by introducing another brand. This is the classic "multibrand" strategy of Procter & Gamble.

It may be a misnomer to call it a multibrand strategy. Rather it's a single-position strategy.

Each brand is uniquely positioned to occupy a certain location in the mind of the prospect. When times change, when new products come and go, no effort is made to change the position. Rather a new product is introduced to reflect changing technologies and changing tastes.

In other words, Procter & Gamble recognizes the enormous difficulty of moving an established position. When you have one already established, why change it? It may be cheaper and more effective in the long run to introduce a new product. Even if you eventually have to kill off an old, established name.

Ivory was a soap. It still is. When heavy-duty laundry detergents became available, the pressure was probably on to introduce Ivory Detergent. But this would have meant changing the position of Ivory in the prospect's mind.

A much better solution was Tide. Now the new detergent concept had a new name to match. And Tide became an enormous success.

And when Procter & Gamble introduced a dishwasher detergent, they didn't call it Dishwasher Tide. They called it Cascade.

Each leading Procter & Gamble brand has its own separate identity: Joy, Crest, Head & Shoulders, Sure, Bounty, Pampers, Comet, Charmin, and Duncan Hines. Not a Plus, Ultra, or Super in the lot.

So a multibrand strategy is really a single-position strategy. One without change. Ivory has been going strong for 99 years.

Covering with a broader name

What dethrones a leader, of course, is change.

The New York Central Railroad was not only the leading railroad in the twenties, it was also the bluest of blue-chip stocks. Several mergers later, the Penn Central (as it is called today) is an anemic relic with scarcely a trace of its former glory.

American Airlines, on the other hand, is flying high.

The covering move for the New York Central, of course, would have been to open an airline division at an early stage in the game.

"What? You want us to start an airline to take business away from our railroad? Over my dead body we will."

The pure covering move is often difficult to sell internally. Management often sees the new product or service as a competitor rather than as an opportunity.

Sometimes a name change will help bridge the gap from one era to the next. By broadening the name, you can allow the company to make the mental transition.

Sales Management changed its name to *Sales & Marketing Management* to encompass the fast-growing function of marketing. At some point in the future the publication could drop the other shoe and change again. To *Marketing Management*.

From Haloid to Haloid Xerox to Xerox is the general pattern.

You know, of course, how the Kodak Company got its name. From Eastman to Eastman Kodak to Kodak, right?

Well, they haven't dropped the other shoe yet. So the official name is still the Eastman Kodak Company.

The Direct Mail Association changed its name a number of years ago to Direct Mail-Marketing Association—a recognition of the fact that mail was only one of the ways for a company to do direct marketing.

So recently they changed again, to the Direct Marketing Association.

While a New York Central Transportation Company might not have been a success either, there is plenty of evidence to indicate that people take names very literally. (Eastern Airlines, for example.)

Government agencies are usually very good at the game of broadening the name. The Department of Housing and Urban Development, for example. (It used to be the Housing and Home Finance Agency.) By broadening the name, a government agency can enlarge its scope of operations, increase its staff, and naturally justify a larger budget.

Oddly enough, one agency that missed a bet was the Federal Trade Commission. A broader name would be Consumer Protection Agency, a name that would also take advantage of a current hot topic.

Leaders can also benefit by broadening the range of applications for their products. Arm & Hammer has done a good job in promoting the use of baking soda in the refrigerator.

The Florida Citrus Commission promotes orange juice, the largest-selling fruit drink, for lunch snacks, with meals, etc. "It isn't just for breakfast anymore," say the commercials.

Business Week, the leading business magazine, has successfully promoted itself as a good publication for consumer advertising. Today roughly 40 percent of its advertising volume is in consumer products.

Leadership is not the end of a positioning program. It's only the start. Leaders are in the best position to exploit opportunites as they arise.

Leaders should constantly use the power of their leadership to keep far ahead of the competition.

7 Positioning of a follower

What works for a leader doesn't necessarily work for a follower. Leaders can often cover a competitive move and retain their leadership.

But followers are not in the same position to benefit from a covering strategy. When a follower copies a leader, it's not covering at all. It's better described as a me-too response. (Usually phrased more diplomatically as "keeping in tune with the times.")

Why products fail

Most products fail to achieve reasonable sales goals because the accent is on "better" rather than "speed." That is, the No. 2 company thinks the road to success is to introduce a me-too product, only better.

It's not enough to be better than the competitor. You must introduce your product before someone else has a chance to establish leadership. With a more massive advertising and promotion launch. And a better name. (More on this point later.)

Yet the opposite normally occurs. The me-too company wastes valuable time on improving the product. Then the launch is made with a smaller advertising budget than the leader's. And then the new product is given the house name, because that's the easy way to ensure a quick share of market. All deadly traps in our overcommunicated society.

How do you find an open position in the prospect's mind?

Cherchez le creneau

The French have a marketing expression that sums up this strategy rather neatly.

Cherchez le creneau. "Look for the hole."

Cherchez le creneau and then fill it.

That advice goes against the "bigger and better" philosophy ingrained into the American spirit.

Another typically American attitude makes positioning thinking difficult. Ever since childhood, we have been taught to think in a certain way.

"The power of positive thinking," Norman Vincent Peale called it. An attitude which may sell a lot of books but which can destroy a person's ability to find a creneau.

To find a creneau, you must have the ability to think in reverse, to go against the grain. If everyone else is going east, see if you can find your creneau by going west. A strategy that worked for Christopher Columbus can also work for you.

Let's explore some strategies for finding creneaus.

The size creneau

For years, Detroit automakers were on a longer, lower kick. Each model year, cars became more streamlined, better looking.

Enter the Volkswagen Beetle. Short, fat, and ugly.

The conventional way to promote the Beetle would have been to minimize the weaknesses and maximize the strengths.

"Let's get a fashion photographer who can make the car look better than it is. Then we'll play up the reliability angle," is your ordinary strategy.

But the creneau was size. The most effective ad Volkswagen ever ran was the one which stated the position clearly and unequivocally.

"Think small."

With two simple words, this headline did two things at once. It stated the Volkswagen position, and it challenged the prospect's assumption that bigger is necessarily better.

The effectiveness of this approach, of course, depends on the existence of an open creneau in the prospect's mind. Not that there weren't other small cars on the market at the time the Beetle was introduced. There were, but no one else had preempted the small-car position.

Integrated circuits and other electronic devices make the "small-size" creneau technically feasible in many product categories. Only time will tell which companies will be able to capitalize on electronics to build valuable positions based on miniaturization.

The opposite presents opportunities too. There are opportunities to build positions in projection television sets and other products based on large size.

The high-price creneau

The classic example is Michelob. The people at Anheuser-Busch found an untapped market for a premium-priced domestic beer. And they moved into the mind with the Michelob name.

High-price creneaus seem to be opening up in many product categories. As our throwaway society sees the urgent need for conversation, there's a new appreciation of a quality product designed to last.

Which is one reason behind the success of $40,000 automobiles like the BMW 635-CS and $50,000 cars like the Mercedes-Benz 500-SEL.

And S. T. Dupont (nice name) lighters at, as the ads say, "$1500 and down."

Price is an advantage, especially if you're the first in the category to establish the high-price creneau.

Some brands base almost their entire product message on the high-price concept.

"There is only one Joy, the costliest perfume in the world."

"Why you should invest in a Piaget, the world's most expensive watch."

High price is effective not only for luxury items like cars, perfume, and watches, but also mundane products like Whitney's Yogurt and Orville Redenbacher's Gourmet Popping Corn.

Mobil 1 synthetic engine lubricant at $3.95 a quart is another example. Even traditional low-priced products like flour, sugar, and salt represent positioning opportunities.

Too often, however, greed gets confused with positioning thinking. Charging high prices is not the way to get rich. Being the first to (1) establish the high-price position (2) with a valid product story (3) in a category where consumers are receptive to a high-priced brand is the secret of success. Otherwise, your high price just drives prospective customers away.

Furthermore, the place to establish the high price is in the ads, not in the store. The price (high or low) is as much a feature of the product as anything else.

If you do your positioning job right, there should be no price surprises in the store. Your ads don't have to quote exact prices, although sometimes that's a good thing to do. What they should do, however, is to clearly position your brand in a particular price category.

The low-price creneau

Instead of high price, the opposite direction can also be a profitable tack to take.

In evaluating price as a possible creneau, keep in mind that the low-price creneau is often a good choice for new products like facsimile equipment and videotape players. Products customers believe they are taking a chance on. (If the thing doesn't work right, I'm not out that much money.)

The high-price creneau is often a good choice for old, established products like automobiles, watches, and television sets. Especially those products for which customers are not happy with existing repair services.

The recent introduction of generic ("no name") food brands is an attempt to exploit the low-price creneau in the supermarket. (Although retailer emphasis on sales and low prices over the years have pretty much wiped out the opportunities in that direction.)

When you combine all three price strategies (high, standard, and low), you normally have a strong marketing approach. As Anheuser-Busch has done with Michelob, Budweiser, and Busch (their low-priced beer).

The weakest brand, of course, is Busch because of the poor name and lack of a strong positioning concept. Why would the owner of the place put his name only on his lowest-priced product?

A better name for a low-priced beer is Old Milwaukee, which leads its category in sales.

Other effective creneaus

Sex is one. Marlboro was the first national brand to establish a masculine position in cigarettes, one reason why Phillip Morris's Marlboro brand has climbed steadily in sales. From fifth place in sales to first place in a 10-year period.

Timing is critical. In 1973 Lorillard tried to introduce its own masculine brand called Luke. The name was terrific, the packaging was great, the advertising was brilliant. "From Kankakee to Kokomo along comes Luke movin' free and slow."

The only thing wrong was the timing. About 20 years too late. Luke really was movin' slow, so Lorillard killed him.

In positioning a product, there's no substitute for getting there first.

What masculinity did for Marlboro, femininity did for Virginia Slims, a brand that carved out a substantial share with the opposite approach. But Eve, a me-too brand that also tried the feminine approach, was a failure. Eve was too late.

When you use sex to segment a product category and establish a position, the obvious approach isn't always the best.

Take perfume, for example. You'd think that the more delicate and feminine the brand, the more successful it would be. So what's the largest-selling brand of perfume in the world?

No, it's not Arpege or Chanel No. 5. It's Revlon's Charlie. The first brand to try a masculine name complete with pantsuit ads.

The knockoff brand, "Just Call Me Maxi," was not only poorly done but reportedly cost the president of Max Factor his job.

The Charlie success story illustrates the paradox of established product categories like perfume. The bulk of the business is in one direction (feminine brand names), but the opportunity lies in the opposite (a masculine brand name).

Age is another positioning strategy to use. Geritol tonic is a good example of a successful product aimed at older folks.

Aim toothpaste is a good example of a product aimed at children. Aim has carved out 10 percent of the toothpaste market. A tremendous accomplishment in a market dominated by two powerful brands, Crest and Colgate.

Time of day is also a potential positioning possibility. Nyquil, the first night-time cold remedy, is one example.

Distribution is another possibility. L'eggs was the first hosiery brand to be distributed in supermarkets and mass merchandise outlets. L'eggs now is the leading brand, with sales in the hundreds of millions.

Another possibility is the heavy-user position. "The one beer to have when you're having more than one" positioned Schaefer as the brand for the heavy beer drinker.

The factory creneau

One common mistake in looking for creneaus is filling a hole in the factory rather than one in the mind.

Ford's Edsel is the classic example. In the laughter that followed the demise of poor Edsel, most people missed the point.

In essence, the Ford people got switched around. The Edsel was a beautiful case of internal positioning to fill a hole between

Ford and Mercury on the one hand and Lincoln on the other hand.

Good strategy inside the factory. Bad strategy outside where there was simply no position for this car in a category already cluttered with heavily chromed, medium-priced cars.

If the Edsel had been tagged a "high-performance" car and presented in a sleek two-door, bucket-seat form and given a name to match, no one would have laughed. It could have occupied a position that no one else owned, and the ending of the story might have been different.

Another "fill-the-factory" mistake was the *National Observer,* the first national weekly newspaper.

Dow Jones, the *Observer's* proud parent, also publishes *The Wall Street Journal,* but only 5 days a week. Voilà, you can hear somebody say. Let's fill the factory with a weekly newspaper. That way, we get free use of those expensive *Journal* presses.

But where was the hole in the prospect's mind? He or she could already subscribe to *Time, Newsweek, U.S. News & World Report,* and other news magazines.

Aah, you say. But the *National Observer* is a weekly newspaper, not a magazine. But that's playing semantic games. Prospects didn't differentiate between the two.

The technology trap

Even a great technical achievement of a research laboratory will fail if there is no creneau in the mind.

In 1971 Brown-Forman Distillers launched Frost 8/80, the first "dry, white whisky."

Frost 8/80 should have been a big success. There was a big hole there. There was no other dry, white whisky. As Brown-Forman president William F. Lucas said, "It was greeted with great applause by our people and a gnashing of teeth by our competitors."

Yet less than 2 years later, Frost 8/80 was dead. A multi-million-dollar failure. Volume had totaled just 100,000 cases, one-third of the company's projections.

What went wrong? Look at the positioning claim from the prospect's point of view.

The first white whisky? Not true. There are at least four others. Their names are gin, vodka, rum, and tequila.

As a matter of fact, Frost 8/80 ads encouraged the prospect to look at the new whisky as a substitute for other distilled spirits. According to the ads, Frost 8/80 could be used like vodka or gin in martinis, like scotch or bourbon in manhattans and whisky sours.

Don't try to trick the prospect. Advertising is not a debate. It's a seduction.

The prospect won't sit still for the finer points of verbal logic. As the politician said, "If it looks like a duck and walks like a duck, I say it's a duck."

The everybody trap

Some marketing people reject the "cherchez le creneau" concept. They don't want to be tied down to a specific position because they believe it limits their sales. Or their opportunities.

They want to be all things to all people.

Years ago, when there were a lot fewer brands and a lot less advertising, it made sense to try to appeal to everybody.

In politics it used to be suicide for a politician to take a strong position on anything. Don't step on anybody's toes.

But today in the product arena and in the political arena, you have to have a position. There are too many competitors out there. You can't win by not making enemies, by being everything to everybody.

To win in today's competitive environment, you have to go out and make friends, carve out a specific niche in the market. Even if you lose a few doing so.

Today the everybody trap may keep you afloat if you're already in office or already own a substantial share of market. But it's deadly if you want to build a position from nowhere.

8 Repositioning the competition

There comes a time when you can't find a creneau. With hundreds of variations in each product category on the market, the chances of finding an open hole today are very slim.

For example, take your average supermarket, with 12,000 different products or brands on display. That means a young person has to sort out and catalog 12,000 different names in his or her head.

When you consider that the average college graduate has a speaking vocabulary of only 8000 words, you can see the problem.

The kid spends 4 years in a university and ends up 4000 words down.

Creating your own creneau

With a plethora of products in every category, how does a company use advertising to blast its way into the mind? The basic underlying marketing strategy has got to be "reposition the competition."

Because there are so few creneaus to fill, a company must create one by repositioning the competitors that occupy the positions in the mind.

In other words, to move a new idea or product into the mind, you must first move an old one out.

"The world is round," said Christopher Columbus. "No, it's not," said the public, "it's flat."

To convince the public otherwise, fifteenth century scientists first had to prove that the world wasn't flat. One of their more convincing arguments was the fact that sailors at sea were first able to observe the tops of the masts of an approaching ship, then the sails, then the hull. If the world were flat, they would see the whole ship at once.

All the mathematical arguments in the world weren't as effective as a simple observation the public could verify themselves.

Once an old idea is overturned, selling the new idea is often ludicrously simple. As a matter of fact, people will often actively search for a new idea to fill the void.

Never be afraid to conflict either. The crux of a repositioning program is undercutting an existing concept, product, or person.

Conflict, even personal conflict, can build a reputation overnight. Where would Sam Ervin have been without Richard Nixon?

For that matter, where would Richard Nixon have been without Alger Hiss?

And Ralph Nader got famous not by saying anything about Ralph Nader but by going out and attacking the world's largest corporation single-handedly.

People like to watch the bubble burst.

Repositioning aspirin

Tylenol went out and burst the aspirin bubble.

"For the millions who should not take aspirin," said Tylenol's ads. "If your stomach is easily upset . . . or you have an ulcer . . . or you suffer from asthma, allergies, or iron-deficiency anemia, it would make good sense to check with your doctor before you take aspirin.

"Aspirin can irritate the stomach lining," continued the Tylenol ad, "trigger asthmatic or allergic reactions, cause small amounts of hidden gastrointestinal bleeding.

"Fortunately, there is Tylenol . . . "

Sixty words of copy before any mention of the advertiser's product.

Sales of Tylenol acetaminophen took off. Today Tylenol is the No. 1 brand of analgesic. Ahead of Anacin. Ahead of Bayer. Ahead of Bufferin. Ahead of Excedrin. A simple but effective repositioning strategy did the job.

Against an institution like aspirin. Amazing.

Repositioning Lenox

For a repositioning strategy to work, you must say something about your competitor's product that causes the prospect to change his or her mind, not about your product, but about the competitor's product.

"Royal Doulton. The china of Stoke-on-Trent, England vs. Lenox. The china of Pomona, New Jersey."

Note how Royal Doulton is repositioning Lenox china, a product that many buyers thought was an imported one. (Lenox. Sounds English, doesn't it?)

Royal Doulton credits a 6 percent gain in market share to this one advertisement.

The late Howard Gossage used to say that the objective of your advertising should not be to communicate with your consumers and prospects at all, but to terrorize your competition's copywriters, and there's some truth in that.

Repositioning American vodkas

"Most American vodkas seem Russian," said the ads. And the captions said: "Samovar: Made in Schenley, Pennsylvania. Smirnoff: Made in Hartford, Connecticut. Wolfschmidt: Made in Lawrenceburg, Indiana.

"Stolichnaya is different. It is Russian," continued the ad. And the bottle is labeled, "Made in Leningrad, Russia."

Stolichnaya sales began to soar as a result. Needless to say.

But why the need to disparage the competition? Couldn't PepsiCo, the importers of the Stolichnaya brand, have simply advertised it as the "Russian vodka?"

They could have, of course. But that presumes a degree of product interest on the part of the vodka buyer that just doesn't exist.

How many times have you picked up a bottle of liquor and read the label to find out where it was made? Furthermore, the names themselves (Samovar, Smirnoff, Wolfschmidt, Popov, Nikolai) imply a Russian origin. It's this latter factor alone that was responsible for much of Stolichnaya's astounding success.

People like to see the high and mighty exposed. Note how other vodka ads play into Stolichnaya's hands.

It was the Golden Age of Russia. Yet in this time when legends lived, the Czar stood like a giant among men. He could bend an iron bar on his bare knee. Crush a silver ruble with his fist. And had a thirst for life like no other man alive. And his drink was Genuine Vodka. Wolfschmidt Vodka.

Then the reader turns the page to find the Stolichnaya ad, where he sees that Wolfschmidt is made in Lawrenceburg, Indiana.

Along comes Afghanistan and suddenly Stolichnaya is in trouble. But only temporarily. After a few months, the storm blew over and Stolichnaya came back bigger than ever.

Repositioning Pringle's

What happened to Pringle's potato chips? Introduced with a $15 million fanfare from Procter & Gamble, the "new-fangled" potato chips rapidly gobbled up 18 percent of the market.

Then the old-fangled brands like Borden's Wise struck back with a classic repositioning strategy.

They read the two labels on television. "In Wise, you find: Potatoes. Vegetable oil. Salt. In Pringle's, you find: Dehydrated potatoes. Mono- and diglycerides. Ascorbic acid. Butylated hydroxy-anisole.''

Sales of Pringle's came tumbling down. From a respectable 18 percent of the potato chip market to 10 percent. A far cry from P & G's goal of 25 percent.

Oddly enough, research isolated another problem. The most common complaint against Pringle's is that they "taste like cardboard.''

It's exactly what you might expect from a consumer exposed to words like "diglycerides" and "butylated hydroxy-anisole." Taste, esthetic or gustatory, is in the mind. Your eyes see what you expect to see. Your tongue reacts the way you expect it to react.

If you were forced to drink a beaker of dihydrogen oxide, your response would probably be negative. If you asked for a glass of water, you might enjoy it.

That's right. There's no difference on the palate. The difference is in the brain.

Recently the Cincinnati giant changed its strategy. Pringle's would become an "all natural" product.

But the damage had already been done. In politics or packaged goods, the rule is once a loser, always a loser. It would be as hard to bring Pringle's back as to bring Jimmy Carter back.

In some small corner of the brain is a penalty box marked "loser." Once your product is sent there, the game is over.

Go back to square one and start all over again. With a new product and a new game.

Of all companies, Procter & Gamble should have known the power of repositioning. And should have taken steps in advance to protect Pringle's.

Repositioning Listerine

One of P & G's most powerful programs is the one for Scope mouthwash. P & G used two words to reposition Listerine, the King of Halitosis Hill.

"Medicine breath."

These two words were enough to torpedo Listerine's highly successful "the taste you hate, twice a day" theme.

The Scope attack carved a few share points out of market leader Listerine and firmly established Scope in second place.

The Listerine/Scope battle caused the usual casualties. Micrin and Binaca folded. Lavoris saw its market share wither away.

But let's face it. Scope has not become the market success it should be, based on theory.

Why? Look at the name again.

Scope? It sounds like a board game from Parker Brothers. Not like a good-tasting mouthwash that will make you a big hit with the opposite sex. If Scope had been given a name like Close-Up toothpaste, it could have parlayed its brilliant repositioning strategy with sales success to match.

Repositioning vs. comparative ads

The success of the Tylenol, Scope, Royal Doulton, and other repositioning programs has spawned a host of similar advertising. Too often, however, these copycat campaigns have missed the essence of repositioning strategy.

"We're better than our competitors" isn't repositioning. It's comparative advertising and not very effective. There's a psychological flaw in the advertiser's reasoning which the prospect is quick to detect. "If your brand is so good, how come it's not the leader?"

A look at comparative ads suggests why most of them aren't effective. They fail to reposition the competition.

Rather, they use the competitor as a benchmark for their own brand. Then they tell the reader or viewer how much better they are. Which, of course, is exactly what the prospect expects the advertiser to say.

"Ban is more effective than Right Guard, Secret, Sure, Arrid Extra Dry, Mitchum, Soft & Dry, Body All, and Dial," said a recent Ban ad. The reader looks at an ad like this and asks, "What else is new?"

Is repositioning legal?

If disparagement were illegal, every politician would be in jail. (And many husbands and wives would be in deep trouble too.)

Actually, the Federal Trade Commission deserves much of the credit for making repositioning ads possible—at least on television.

In 1964 the National Broadcasting Company dropped its ban on comparative advertising. But nothing much happened. Commercials are expensive to produce, a few advertisers wanted to produce two versions. One to run on NBC and one to run on the other two networks.

So in 1972 the FTC prodded the American Broadcasting Company and the Columbia Broadcasting System to allow commercials that named rival brands.

In 1974 the American Association of Advertising Agencies issued new comparative ad guidelines which represented a complete turnaround from previous policy. Traditionally, the 4A's had discouraged the use of comparative ads by its member agencies.

In 1975 the Independent Broadcasting Authority, which controls radio and television in Britain, gave the green light for "knocking" ads in the U.K.

So repositioning has been "legal" for at least a decade

Is repositioning ethical?

In the past advertising was prepared in isolation. That is, you studied the product and its features, and then you prepared advertising which communicated to your customers and prospects the benefits of those features. It didn't make much difference whether the competition offered those features or not.

In the traditional approach, you ignored competition and made every claim seem like a preemptive claim. Mentioning a competitive product, for example, was considered not only bad taste but poor strategy as well.

In the positioning era, however, the rules are reversed. To establish a position, you must often not only name competitive names but also ignore most of the old advertising rules as well.

In category after category, the prospect already knows the benefits of using the product. To climb on his or her product ladder, you must relate your brand to the brands already in the prospect's mind.

Yet repositioning programs, even though effective, have stirred up a host of complaints. Many advertising people deplore the use of such tactics.

An old-time advertising man put it this way. "Times have changed. No longer are advertisers content to huckster their own wares on their own merits. Their theme now is how much better their product is than any other. It is a deplorable situation, with TV as the worst offender, where competitive products are pictured and denigrated before the eyes of millions. There should be some kind of regulation to restrict that type of unethical marketing."

"Comparative advertising is not against the law," said the chairman of a top 10 agency, "nor should it be. But to practice it as we do today makes a mockery of pretensions to culture and refinement and decent corporate behavior."

You can't have it both ways. If you want culture and refinement, you produce operas. If you want to make money, you produce movies.

Culture and refinement may be admirable qualities, but not in advertising.

Is society sick when people are ready to believe the worst about a product or person, but balk about believing the best?

Are newspapers wrong to put the bad news on the front page and the good news in the back along with the society columns? (If they print any at all.)

The communication industry is like gossip. It feeds on the bad news, not the good.

It may not be your idea of the way things should be. It just happens to be the way things are.

To be successful in this overcommunicated society of ours, you have to play the game by the rules that society sets. Not your own.

Don't be discouraged. A little disparagement may be preferable in the long run to a lot of conventional "brag and boast."

Done honestly and fairly, it keeps the competition on their toes.

9

The power of the name

The name is the hook that hangs the brand on the product ladder in the prospect's mind. In the positioning era, the single most important marketing decision you can make is what to name the product.

Shakespeare was wrong. A rose by any other name would not smell as sweet. Not only do you see what you want to see, you also smell what you want to smell. Which is why the single most important decision in the marketing of perfume is the name you decide to put on the brand.

Would "Alfred" have sold as well as "Charlie?" Don't bet on it.

And Hog Island in the Caribbean was going nowhere until they changed the name to Paradise Island.

How to choose a name

Don't look to the past for guidance and pick the name of a French racing car driver (Chevrolet) or the daughter of your Paris representative (Mercedes).

What worked in the past won't necessarily work now or in the future. In the past when there were fewer products, when the volume of communication was lower, the name wasn't nearly as important.

Today, however, a lazy, say-nothing name isn't good enough to cut into the mind. What you must look for is a name that begins the positioning process, a name that tells the prospect what the product's major benefit is.

Like Head & Shoulders shampoo, Intensive Care skin lotion, and Close-Up toothpaste.

Or like DieHard for a longer-lasting battery. Shake 'n Bake for a new way to cook chicken. Edge for a shaving cream that lets you shave closer.

A name should not go "over the edge," though. That is, become so close to the product itself that it becomes generic, a general name for all products of its class rather than a trade name for a specific brand.

"Lite beer from Miller" is a typical product name that went over the line. So now we have Schlitz Light, Coors Light, Bud Light, and a host of other light beers. The public and the press quickly corrupted the name to "Miller Lite," and so Miller lost its right to exclusive use of "light" or its phonetic equivalent as a trademark for beer.

For years to come, trademark attorneys will be using Lite as an example of the danger of using descriptive words as trademarks. (Lawyers love coined names like Kodak and Xerox.)

Choosing a name is like driving a racing car. To win, you have to take chances. You have to select names that are almost, but not quite, generic. If once in a while you go off the track into generic territory, so be it. No world champion driver has made it to the top without spinning out a few times.

A strong, generic-like, descriptive name will block your me-too competitors from muscling their way into your territory. A good name is the best insurance for long-term success. *People* is a brilliant name for the gossip-column magazine. It's a runaway success. The me-too copy, *Us* magazine, is in trouble.

How not to choose a name

On the other hand. *Time* is not as good a name for a newsweekly as the more generic *Newsweek*.

Time was the first into the newsweekly pool and is an obvious success. But *Newsweek* isn't far behind. (As a matter of fact, *Newsweek* sells more pages of advertising each year than does *Time*.)

Many people think *Time* is a great name for a magazine. And in a way, it is. Short, catchy, memorable. But it's also subtle and tricky. (*Time* could be a trade magazine for the watch industry.)

Fortune is another name cut out of the same cloth. (*Fortune* could be a magazine for stockbrokers, commodity traders, or gamblers. It's not clear.) *Business Week* is a much better name. Also a more successful magazine.

Names also get out of date, opening up creneaus for alert competitors.

Esquire was a great name for a magazine for the young-man-about-town. When young-men-about-town used to sign their names John J. Smith, Esq. But *Esquire* lost its leadership to *Playboy*. Everybody knows what a playboy is and what he's interested in. Girls, right? But what's an esquire? And what's he interested in?

For many years, *Yachting* has been the leading publication in the marine field. But today how many esquires own yachts? So every year *Sail Magazine* keeps getting closer in sales to *Yachting*.

When virtually all advertising was in newspapers and magazines, *Printer's Ink* was a good name for a magazine directed to the advertising field. But today radio and television are just as important as print. So *Printer's Ink* is dead and *Advertising Age* reigns supreme.

One of the strongest publications in the world today is *The Wall Street Journal*. It has no real competitors. But *The Wall Street Journal* is a weak name for a daily business newspaper. The name implies a narrow, financial orientation. But the publication covers business generally.

Of such observations are opportunities fashioned.

Engineers and scientists in love with their own creations are responsible for some of the really bad names. Names like XD-12, for example. (Presumably standing for "experimental design number 12.") These are inside jokes that have no meaning in the mind of the prospect.

Take Mennen E, for example. People are literal and they take things literally. Mennen E deodorant was doomed to failure in spite of a $10 million advertising launch. The trouble was the name on the can. The introductory ad even admitted that the idea was a little unusual. "Vitamin E, incredibly, is a deodorant."

It is incredible. That is, unless they were appealing to people who want the strongest, best-fed, healthiest armpits in the country. Mennen E didn't last very long.

And what about Breck One and Colgate 100? Brand names like these are meaningless.

With marginal differences in many product categories, a better name can mean millions of dollars difference in sales.

When to use a coined name

What about the obvious success of companies with coined names like Coca-Cola, Kodak, and Xerox?

One of the things that makes positioning thinking difficult for many people is the failure to understand the role of timing.

The first company into the mind with a new product or new idea is going to become famous. Whether the name is Lindbergh or Smith or Rumplestiltskin.

Coca-Cola was first with a cola drink. Kodak was first with low-cost photography. Xerox was first with the plain-paper copier.

Take the word "Coke." Because of the success of Coca-Cola, the nickname Coke has acquired what the semanticists call a secondary meaning.

Would you name a soft drink after the word for "the residue of coal burned in the absence of air"? Or the street name for a narcotic cocaine?

So strong is the secondary meaning of the word Coke that the Coca-Cola Company has nothing to fear from these negative connotations.

But choosing a coined name like Keds, Kleenex, and Kotex for a new product is dangerous, to say the least. Only when you are first in the mind with an absolutely new product that millions of people are certain to want can you afford the luxury of a mean-nothing name.

Then, of course, any name would work.

So stick with common descriptive words (Spray 'n Wash) and avoid the coined words (Qyx).

As a guide, the five most common initial letters are S, C, P, A, and T. The five least common are X, Z, Y, Q, and K. One out of eight English words starts with an S. One out of 3000 starts with an X.

Negative names can be positive

Technology continues to create new and improved products. Yet they often are scarred at birth with second-class imitation names.

Take margarine, for example. Even though the product has been around for decades, it is still perceived as imitation butter. (It's not nice to fool Mother Nature.)

A better choice of name at the beginning would have helped. What should margarine have been called? Why "soy butter," of course—a name in the peanut butter tradition.

The psychological problem with a name like "margarine" is that it is deceptive. It hides the origin of the product.

Everyone knows that butter is made from milk. But what's margarine made from? Because the origin of the product is hidden, the prospect assumes there must be something basically wrong with margarine.

Bringing the product out of the closet

The first step in overcoming negative reactions is to bring the product out of the closet. To deliberately polarize the situation by using a negative name like soy butter.

Once this is done, it allows the development of a long-term program to sell the advantages of soy butter vs. cow butter. An essential ingredient of such a program is "pride of origin" which the soy name connotes.

The same principle is involved in the shift from colored to Negro to black.

"Negro" is a margarine name, forever relating Negroes to second-class citizenship. "Colored" doesn't sufficiently polarize the situation. The implication is, the less colored the better.

"Black" is a much better choice. It allows the development of "pride of blackness," an essential first step to long-term equality. (You might prefer to be white, but I prefer to be black.)

In naming people or products, you should not let your competitors unfairly preempt words that you need to describe your own products. Like butter in the case of margarine. Or like sugar in the case of corn syrup.

A number of years ago, scientists found a way to make sweeteners out of corn starch. Result: products called dextrose, corn syrup, and high-fructose corn syrup.

With names like "high-fructose corn syrup," it's no wonder that even in the trade the products were considered imitation or second-class in comparison with sucrose or "real sugar." So Corn Products, one of the major suppliers of corn syrups, decided to call its sweeteners "corn sugars." This move allowed the company to put corn on an equal footing with cane and beet.

"Consider all three types of sugar," say the ads. "Cane, beet, and corn."

Marketing people should know that the Federal Trade Commission is the keeper of the generics for many industries. But the FTC can be persuaded. "If we can't call it sugar, can we put corn syrup in a soft drink and call the product 'sugar-free'?"

Special-interest groups recognize the power of a good name. The "Right to Life" movement and "fair trade" laws are two examples.

And what senator or representative would dare oppose a bill called the "Clean Air Act?"

In working against an established concept like "fair trade," it's important not to try to rename the competition. All you cause is confusion among your audience.

To counter the widespread consumer acceptance of fair trade laws, the opposition tried to call it "price maintenance" legislation. It was many, many years before fair trade laws were repealed by the many states that had enacted them.

A better tactic is to turn the name around. That is to reposition the concept by using the same words to turn the meaning inside out. "Fair to the trade, but unfair to the consumer" is an example of this tactic.

Even better is to rename the opposition before the powerful name takes root. "Price manitenance" would probably have worked as a blocking strategy, but only early in the game. Another example of the importance of being first.

David and Michael and Hubert and Elmer

In spite of the common belief that it's "only a name," there is a growing body of evidence that a person's name plays a significant role in the game of life.

Two psychology professors, Dr. Herbert Harari and Dr. John W. McDavid, were trying to find out why elementary school students made fun of classmates with unusual names.

So they experimented with different names attributed to compositions supposedly written by fourth and fifth graders. Two sets of names, in particular, illustrate the principle.

There were two popular names (David and Michael) and two unpopular names (Hubert and Elmer) on some of the compositions. Each composition was given to a different group of elementary school teachers to grade. (The teachers that participated in the experiment had no reason to believe they weren't grading ordinary school papers.)

Would you believe that compositions bearing the names of David and Michael averaged a letter grade higher than the same compositions attributed to Elmer and Hubert? "Teachers know from past experience," say the professors, "that a Hubert or an Elmer is generally a loser."

What about famous people with odd first names? Hubert Humphrey and Adlai Stevenson, for example. Both losers to men with the popular names of Richard and Dwight.

What if Richard Humphrey had run against Hubert Nixon? Would America have elected a Hubert Nixon?

Jimmy, Jerry, Richard, Lyndon, John, Dwight, Harry, Franklin. Not since Herbert have we had a "loser" name in the White House.

And who did Herbert Hoover beat in 1928? Another man with a loser name, Alfred.

In 1932, when Herbert ran against a "winner" name like Franklin, he lost. And he lost big.

What would you expect from someone named Edsel? Edsel was a loser name before Ford introduced the Edsel car. And the name contributed to the marketing disaster.

Take Cyril and John. According to psychologist David Sheppard, people who don't know anyone with these names nevertheless expect a Cyril to be sneaky and a John to be trustworthy.

You see what you expect to see. And a bad or inappropriate name sets up a chain reaction that only serves to confirm your initial unfavorable opinion.

Elmer is a loser. See, he's not doing that job very well. I told you, Elmer is a loser.

A true story. An account officer at a New York bank was named Young J. Boozer. Once when a customer asked to speak to "Young Boozer," he was told by the switchboard operator, "We have a lot of them around here. Which one do you want to talk to?"

Hubert and Elmer in the sky

The name is the first point of contact between the message and the mind.

It's not the goodness or badness of the name in an esthetic sense that determines the effectiveness of the message. It's the appropriateness of the name.

Take the airline industry, for example. The four largest domestic carriers are United, American, Delta and . . .

Well, do you know the name of the "second largest passenger carrier of all the airlines in the free world," to use one of the airline's advertising slogans?

That's right. Eastern Airlines.

Like all airlines, Eastern has had its ups and downs. Unfortunately, more downs than ups. Among the four largest domestic airlines, Eastern consistently ranks fourth on passenger surveys.

Why? Eastern has a regional name that puts it in a different category in the prospect's mind than big nationwide names like American and United.

The name Eastern puts the airline in the same category with Piedmont, Ozark, and Southern.

You see what you expect to see. The passenger who has a bad experience on American or United says, "It was just one of those things." An exception to the good service he or she was expecting.

The passenger who has a bad experience on Eastern says, "It's that Eastern Airlines again." A continuation of the bad service he or she was expecting.

It's not that Eastern hasn't tried. A number of years ago, Eastern brought in some big-league marketing people and pulled out the throttle. Eastern was among the first to "paint the planes," "improve the food," and "dress up the flight attendants" in an effort to improve its reputation.

And Eastern hasn't been bashful when it comes to spending money. Year after year, it has one of the biggest advertising budgets in the industry. In a recent year, Eastern spent more than $70 million on advertising.

For all the money, what do you think of Eastern? Where do you think they fly? Up and down the East Coast, to New York, Boston, Philadelphia, Washington, Miami, right?

Well, Eastern also goes to St. Louis, New Orleans, Atlanta, Denver, Los Angeles, Seattle, Acapulco, Mexico City.

You can't hang "the wings of man" on a regional name. When prospects are given a choice, they are going to prefer the national airline, not the regional one.

The airline's problem is typical of the difficulty people have in separating reality from perception. Many experienced marketing people look at the Eastern situation and say, "It's not the name that gets Eastern into trouble. It's the poor service, the food, the baggage handling, the surly flight attendants." The perception is the reality.

What do you think of Piedmont Airlines? How about Ozark Airlines? And what about Allegheny?

Allegheny, of course, has thrown in the towel and become USAir. Even North Central and Southern gave up and merged to become Republic Airlines. Both airlines are doing quite well.

The Akron twins

Another common name problem is represented by two companies headquartered in Akron, Ohio.

What does a company do when its name (Goodrich) is similar to the name of a larger company in the same field (Goodyear)?

Goodrich has problems. Research indicates that they could reinvent the wheel and Goodyear would get most of the credit.

Not surprisingly, B. F. Goodrich recognizes the problem. This is how they expressed it a number of years ago in an advertisement:

> The curse of Benjamin Franklin Goodrich. His name. It's one of fate's cruel accidents that our biggest competitor's name turns out to be almost identical to our founder's. Goodyear. Goodrich. Awfully confusing.

At the bottom of the ad, it says: "If you want Goodrich, you'll just have to remember Goodrich."

In other words, it's not Goodrich's problem at all. It's your problem.

B. F. Goodrich was the first domestic company to market steel-belted radial-ply tires in the United States. Yet several years later when tire buyers were asked which company makes steel-belted radials, 56 percent named Goodyear, which didn't make them for the domestic market. Only 47 percent said Goodrich, which did.

As they say in Akron, "Goodrich invents it. Firestone develops it. Goodyear sells it."

Every year Goodyear increases its lead. Today it outsells Goodrich 3 to 1. So the rich get richer. Fair enough.

But what is odd is that the loser's advertising continues to get all the publicity. "We're the other guys" got a lot of favorable attention in the press. But not a lot of favorable attention from the tire-buying public. Its name alone forever condemns Goodrich to eat the dust of its bigger competitor.

The Toledo triplets

If the Akron twins seem confusing, consider the predicament of the Toledo triplets. Owens-Illinois, Owens-Corning Fiberglas and Libbey-Owens-Ford.

These are not small outfits either. Owens-Illinois is a $3.5 billion company. Owens-Corning Fiberglas is a $3 billion company. And Libbey-Owens-Ford is a $1.75 billion company.

Look at the confusion problem from the point of view of Owens-Corning Fiberglas.

Owens, of course, is usually connected with Illinois. Owens-Illinois is a larger company with a stronger claim to the Owens name.

And Corning is usually linked with glass. In nearby Corning, New York, is the Corning Glass Works, a $1.7 billion company. It has succeeded in firmly linking the Corning name to the glass concept.

So what's left for Owens-Corning Fiberglas?

Fiberglas.

Which is probably why the company runs ads that say "Owens-Corning is Fiberglas." In other words, if you want Fiberglas, you'll just have to remember Owens-Corning.

It would be a lot easier if the company changed its name to the Fiberglas Corporation. Then if you want fiberglass (with a lowercase "f"), all you have to remember is Fiberglas (with an uppercase "F"). This step would help focus the attention on the company's primary objective, to turn fiberglass from a generic name back into a brand name.

What should you do if your name is Hubert or Elmer or Eastern or Goodrich or Owens-Corning Fiberglas? Change it.

But name changing is rare, in spite of the logic. Most companies are convinced they have too much equity in their present name. "Our customers and employees would never accept a new name."

What about Olin and Mobil and Uniroyal and Xerox? And how about Exxon Corporation? It was only a few years ago that Exxon changed its name from. . . .

Well, do you even remember what Exxon's old name was? No, it wasn't Esso and it wasn't Humble Oil or Enjay, although the company did use these names in its marketing operations.

The old name of Exxon Corporation was Standard Oil of New Jersey. Amazing what a few years and a few dollars can do.

There is only negative equity in a bad name. When the name is bad, things tend to get worse. When the name is good, things tend to get better.

Continental confusion

Do you know the difference between a $4.6 billion company called The Continental Group, Inc., and a $4 billion company called The Continental Corporation? Not too many people do until they find out that The Continental Group is the world's largest maker of cans and Continental Corporation is the big insurance company.

"Ah, yes. Continental Can and Continental Insurance. Now I know the companies you meant."

Why would a company drop "can" and "insurance" in favor of the anonymity of "group" and "corporation"? The obvious answer is that these two companies sell more than cans and insurance.

But is it possible to build an identity on a nothing name? Unlikely, especially when you consider the existence of other companies with claims on the Continental name. There is Continental Oil, Continental Telephone, Continental Grain, and Continental Illinois Corp. (All billion dollar companies, by the way.)

Or how about the secretary whose boss says, "Get me Continental on the phone." In Manhattan alone, there are 235 listings in the telephone directory starting with Continental.

10 The no-name trap

"I'm going to L.A.," the corporate executive will say. "And then I have to make a trip to New York." Why is Los Angeles often called L.A., but New York is seldom called N.Y.?

"I worked for GE for a couple of years and then went to Western Union." Why is General Electric often called GE, but Western Union is seldom called WU?

General Motors is often GM, American Motors is often AM, but Ford Motor is almost never FM.

Phonetic shorthand

The principle at work here is phonetic shorthand.

Ra-di-o Cor-po-ra-tion of A-mer-i-ca is 12 syllables long. No wonder most people use R-C-A, three syllables long.

Gen-er-al E-lec-tric is six syllables long, so most people use G-E, two syllables.

Gen-er-al Mo-tors is often GM. A-mer-i-can Mo-tors is often AM. But Ford Mo-tor is almost never referred to as FM. The single syllable Ford says it all.

But where there's no phonetic advantage, most people won't use initials. New York and N.Y. are both two syllables long. So while the initials N.Y. are often written, they are seldom spoken.

Los An-ge-les is four syllables long, so L.A. is frequently used. Note, too, that San Fran-cis-co, a four-syllable word, is seldom shortened to "S.F." Why? There's a perfectly good two-syllable word (Frisco) to use a shorthand for San Francisco. Which is why people say "Jer-sey" for New Jersey instead of "N.J."

When they have a choice of a word or a set of initials, both equal in phonetic length, people will invariably use the word, not the initials.

Phonetic length can sometimes fool you. The initials WU look a lot shorter than the name Western Union. But phoneti-cally they are exactly the same length. Dou-ble-U U. West-ern Un-ion. (Except for W, every other English language letter is just one syllable.)

While customers refer to companies phonetically, the com-panies they talk about have a different way of looking at them-selves. Companies are visually oriented. They go to a lot of trou-ble making sure the names look right without considering how it sounds.

Visual shorthand

Business people also fall into the same trap. The first thing to go is the given name. When young Edmund Gerald Brown starts up the executive ladder at General Manufacturing Cor-poration, he instantly becomes E. G. Brown from GMC on internal letters and memos.

But to be well known, you've got to avoid using initials—a fact known by most politicians. Which is why E. M. Kennedy and J. E. Carter bill themselves as Ted Kennedy and Jimmy Carter.

As a matter of fact, the new wave of politicians don't use either middle names or initials. Jack Kemp, Gary Hart, Bill Bradley, George Bush, Ronald Reagan.

What about FDR and JFK? The irony of the situation is that once you get to the top, once you are well known, then initials can be used without ambiguity. Franklin Delano Roosevelt and

John Fitzgerald Kennedy could use initials only after they became famous. Not before.

The next thing to go is the name of the company. What starts out as visual shorthand to conserve paper and typing time ends up as the monogram of success.

IBM, AT&T, GE, 3M. Sometimes it seems that membership in the Fortune 500 depends upon having a readily recognized set of initials. The moniker that tells the world you have made it.

So today, we have such monikers as AM International, AMAX, AMF, AMP, BOC, CBI Industries, CF Industries, CPC International, EG&G, FMC, GAF, IC Industries, ITT, LTV, MEI, NCR, NL Industries, NVF, PPG Industries, SCM, TRW, and VF.

These are not two-bit companies. All are currently on *Fortune's* list of the 500 largest industrial companies. The smallest company on the list, AM International, had sales of $598 million in a recent year and more than 10,000 employees. (You might recognize them as the former Addressograph Multigraph Corp.)

If you select the company next up in size from every initial company on the Fortune 500 list, you will find the following: Allegheny International, American Motors, Amstar, Bristol-Myers, Celanese, Cluett Peabody, Consolidated Foods, Data General, Gannett, Hartmarx, H. J. Heinz, Hewlett-Packard, Inspiration Resources, Lever Brothers, Louisiana Land & Exploration, Mohasco, National Cooperative Refinery Association, North American Philips, Procter & Gamble, G. D. Searle, Weirton Steel, and Westmoreland Coal.

Which list of companies is better known? The name companies, of course.

Some of the initial companies like ITT and NCR are well known, to be sure. But like FDR and JFK, these companies were well known before they dropped their names in favor of initials.

Which companies are likely to grow faster? Again, the name companies.

To test this point, we conducted a survey of both "name" and "initial" companies using a *Business Week* subscriber list. The results show the value of a name.

The average awareness of the "initial" companies was 49 percent. The average awareness of a matched group of "name" companies was 68 percent, 19 percentage points higher.

What drives big companies into committing corporate suicide? For one thing, the top executives have seen the company's initials on internal memos for so long they just naturally assume that everybody knows good old VF. Then, too, they misread the reasons for the success of companies like IBM and GE.

No shortcuts to success

A company must be extremely well known before it can use initials successfully. Apparently the use of the initials "GE" triggers the words "General Electric" inside the brain.

Invariably, people must know the name first before they will respond to initials. The Federal Bureau of Investigation and the Internal Revenue Service are extremely well known. So we respond instantly to FBI and IRS.

But HUD is not recognized nearly so quickly. Why? Because most people don't know the Department of Housing and Urban Development. So if HUD wants to become better known, the department must first make the name Housing and Urban Development better known. Taking a shortcut by using only the initials HUD won't help very much.

Similarly, General Aniline & Film was not a very well known company. When they changed their name to GAF, they made certain that they were never going to become very well known. Now that GAF has legally changed its name to initials, presumably there's no way to expose the prospect to the original name.

Yet alphabet soup seems to be on the corporate menu of many companies today. They fail to think through the process of positioning themselves in the mind. So they fall victim to the fad of the day.

And, no question about it, today's fad is "initialitus." Look at RCA. Everyone knows that RCA stands for Radio Corporation of America. So the company could use the initials to trigger the "Radio Corporation of America" words buried deep inside the mind.

But now that RCA is legally RCA, what will happen next? Nothing. At least in the next decade or so. The words are already buried in the minds of millions of people. And they'll stay there indefinitely.

But what about the next generation of prospects? What will they think when they see those strange initials, RCA?

Roman Catholic Archdiocese?

Positioning is like the game of life. A long-term proposition. Name decisions made today may not bear fruit until many, many years in the future.

The mind works by ear

The primary reason name selection errors are so common is that executives live in an ocean of paper. Letters, memos, reports. Swimming in the Xerox sea, it's easy to forget that the mind works aurally. To utter a word, we first translate the letters into sounds. Which is why beginners move their lips when they read.

When you were a child, you first learned to speak and then to read. And you learned to read slowly and laboriously by saying the words out loud as you forced your mind to connect the written word with the aural sound stored in the brain.

By comparison, learning to speak requires much less effort than learning to read. We store sounds directly and then play them back in various combinations as our mental dexterity improves.

As you grow up, you learn to translate written words into the aural language needed by the brain so rapidly that you are unaware the translation process is taking place.

Then you read in the paper that 80 percent of learning takes place through the eyes. Of course it does. But reading is only a portion of the learning process. Much learning occurs from visual clues which do not involve reading in the conventional sense at all. As when you learn the emotional state of another person by "reading" body clues.

When words are read, they are not understood until the visual/verbal translator in your brain takes over to make aural sense out of what you have seen.

In the same way, a musician learns to read music and hear the sound in his or her head, just as if someone were actually playing the tune on an instrument.

Try to memorize a poem without reading it out loud. It's far easier to memorize written material if we reinforce the aural component, the working language of the brain.

Which is why not only names but also headlines, slogans, and themes should be examined for their aural qualities. Even if you plan to use them in printed material only.

Did you think that Hubert and Elmer were bad names? If so, you must have translated the printed words into their aural equivalents. Because Hubert and Elmer don't look bad. They just sound bad.

In a way, it's a shame that the print media (newspapers, magazines, outdoor advertising) came first and radio second. Radio is really the primal media. And print is the higher-level abstraction.

Messages would "sound better" in print if they were designed for radio first. Yet we usually do the reverse. We work first in print and then in the broadcast media.

Name obsolescence

Another reason companies drop their names for initials is the obsolescence of the name itself. RCA sells a lot of things besides radios.

And how about United Shoe Machinery? The company had become a conglomerate. Furthermore, the domestic shoe machinery market was drying up as imports continually increased their share. What to do? They took the easy way out.

United Shoe Machinery changed its name to USM Corporation. And lived anonymously ever after.

Smith-Corona-Marchant is another company which has lost its corporate identity. The result of mergers, Smith never did make coronas or marchants. So it decided to shorten the name to SCM Corporation.

Presumably, both SCM and USM made the change to escape the obsolete identity of the past. Yet the fact is that the exact opposite occurred.

The mind can't remember USM without dredging United Shoe Machinery from it subconscious.

At least RCA, USM, and SCM had phonetic shorthand going for them. Without it, the difficulties are greater. Much, much greater. When Corn Products Company changed its name to CPC International, it found little recognition of the CPC name. The initials CPC are not phonetically shorter than Corn Products. Both are three syllables long, so the CPC initials were seldom used until the name change was made. Ask people in the business if they are familiar with CPC International. See if they don't say, "Oh, you mean Corn Products Company?"

In our initial-happy society, the first question the mind normally asks itself is, "What do those initials stand for?"

The mind sees the letters AT&T and says, "Ah, American Telephone & Telegraph."

But what reply does the mind get when it sees TRW? Obviously, there are a fair number of people who remember the Thompson Ramo Wooldridge Corporation. And TRW is a $6 billion company, so it gets a lot of press and does a lot of advertising. But would those advertising dollars work harder if TRW had a "name" name instead of an initial name?

Some companies put sets of initials in series. How about trying to remember the D-M-E Corporation, a subsidiary of VSI Corporation?

We're not trying to suggest that companies shouldn't change their names. Quite the contrary. Nothing remains the same for very long. Times change. Products become obsolete.

Markets come and go. And mergers are often necessary. So the time comes when a company must change its name.

U.S. Rubber was a worldwide corporation that marketed many products not made of rubber. Eaton Yale & Towne was the result of a merger that produced a big company with a complicated name. Socony-Mobil was saddled with a first name that originally stood for Standard Oil Company of New York.

All of these names have been changed for sound marketing reasons. The traditional "foot-in-the-past" approach could have produced USR Corporation, EY&T Company, and SM Inc. Three marketing monstrosities.

Instead, "forgetting the past" created three new modern corporate identities—Uniroyal, Eaton, and Mobil. The marketing strengths of these names speak for themselves. These companies successfully forgot the past and positioned themselves against the future.

The confusion between cause and effect

In spite of the drawbacks, companies are lured to initials like moths to a candle. The success of the IBMs of this world seems to be proof that initials are effective. It's the classic confusion between cause and effect.

International Business Machines became so rich and famous (the cause) that everyone knew what company you were talking about when you used its initials (the effect).

When you try to reverse the procedure, it doesn't work. You can't use the initials of a company that is only modestly successful (the cause) and then expect it to become rich and famous (the effect).

It's like trying to become rich and famous by buying limousines and corporate jets. First, you have to become successful in order to have the money to buy the fringe benefits.

In some ways, the rush to adopt initials represents a desire to look accepted even at the cost of a loss in communications. It also represents the copycat thinking prevalent in some management circles. The success of IBM encouraged word processing competitors like CPT and NBI to use initials in their names.

The success of AT&T encouraged MCI to also market their long distance service with an initial name.

And look at the contrasting name strategies of two different airlines.

Pan A-mer-i-can Air-lines (seven syllables) has a phonetically long name. So they shortened it to Pan Am, two syllables. Much better than the initials PAA, which would be difficult to remember.

Trans World Air-lines (four syllables) is actually phonetically shorter than the T-Dou-ble-U-A they are using, But isn't TWA well known? Yes, it is, thanks to $70 million worth of advertising a year.

Although TWA spends about as much on advertising as its larger American and United competitors, surveys show that TWA has half the passenger preference of the other two. The inefficiency of the initials TWA is one reason.

What name should Trans World Airlines use?

"Trans World," of course. Only two syllables long, Trans World is short and graphic.

Acronyms and phone directories

Some companies are lucky. Their initials, either by design or by accident, form acronyms. For example: Fiat (Federation International Automobiles Torino) and Sabena (*Société Anonyme Belge d'Exploitation de la Navigation Aeriènne*).

Often organizations will select carefully names that form meaningful acronyms. Two examples: CARE (Committee for Aid and Rehabilitation in Europe) and MADD (Mothers Against Drunk Drivers).

Other companies aren't so lucky. When General Aniline & Film changed its name to GAF, it chose to overlook the fact that the acronym sounds like "clumsy error." GAF is a gaffe in more ways than one.

The other thing people tend to forget when they pick a name is the problem of finding it in the telephone directory. Since you seldom look up your own name in a phone book, you might not realize how hard it is to locate.

Take MCI, for example. In the Manhattan telephone directory, you might expect to find MCI somewhere between McHugh and McKensie. But of course, it's not there. MCI Telecommunications is 48 pages away where it has to compete with seven other companies that incorporate MCI in their names. (Following standard rules of alphabetizing a list of names, the phone company puts all initial names up front.)

Take USM Corporation, for example. In the Manhattan telephone directory, there are seven pages of listings starting with "US." So you ought to be able to find USM somewhere between US Luggage & Leather Products and *US News & World Report*.

But, of course, it's not there. Those US listings stand for "United States," as in United States Luggage. The US in USM doesn't stand for anything. So again the name goes up front with the rest of the "pure" initial companies.

Many companies are saddled with obsolete names through no fault of their own. But before you throw away a name in favor of meaningless initials, see if you can find another "name" that will do the job you want done.

With a good name, your positioning job is going to be a lot easier.

11 The free-ride trap

Take a product called Alka-Seltzer Plus. Let's see if we can visualize how Alka-Seltzer Plus might have gotten its name.

A bunch of the boys are sitting around a conference table trying to name a new cold remedy designed to compete with Dristan and Contac.

"I have it," says Harry. "Let's call it Alka-Seltzer Plus. That way we can take advantage of the $20 million a year we're already spending on the Alka-Seltzer name."

"Good thinking, Harry," and another money-saving idea is instantly accepted, as most money-saving ideas usually are.

But lo and behold, instead of eating into the Dristan and Contac market, the new product turns around and eats into the Alka-Seltzer market.

Every so often the makers of Alka-Seltzer Plus redesign the label. The "Alka-Seltzer" gets smaller and smaller, and the "Plus" gets bigger and bigger.

A better name for the product would have been Bromo-Seltzer Plus. That way they could have taken business away from the competition.

The conglomeration of the corporation

In the product era life was simpler. Each company specialized in a single line. The name told it all.

Standard Oil, U.S. Steel, U.S. Rubber, United Airlines, Pennsylvania Railroad.

But technological progress created opportunities. So companies started branching into new fields.

Enter the conglomerate. The company that specializes in nothing. By development or acquisition, the conglomerate is prepared to enter any field in which it thinks it can make a buck.

Take General Electric. GE makes everything from jet engines to nuclear power plants to plastics.

RCA is in satellite communications, solid-state electronics, and rent-a-cars.

Many people pooh-pooh the conglomerate. Companies should "stick to their knitting," they say. But conglomerates have provided the capital to sustain vigorous competition in the marketplace. If it weren't for the conglomerates, we would be a nation of semimonopolies.

Take copiers, for example. Xerox, the pioneer in the plain-paper field, now faces competition from the computer manufacturer (IBM), from a photo company (Kodak), and from a postage-meter company (Pitney Bowes).

Even when conglomerates grow by acquisition (RCA's purchase of Hertz, ITT's purchase of Avis), they provide the money needed to sustain growth and competition.

Otherwise, when the original founders retired or died, the tax bite would leave the company too weak to defend its turf.

The typical life cycle of a corporation starts with an entrepreneur with an idea. If successful, you can count on two things, death and taxes, to ensure that the operation will end up as part of a conglomerate.

Two different strategies

Because companies grow by two different strategies (internal development or external acquisition), two different "name" strategies evolved. Corporate egos dictate the strategies.

When a company develops a product internally, it usually puts the corporate name on the product. For example, General Electric computers.

When the company develops a product by external acquisition, it usually keeps the existing name. RCA kept the Hertz name. ITT kept the Avis name.

But not always.

When Sperry-Rand developed a computer line internally, they called the product Univac. When Xerox went into computers by external acquisition, they changed the name from Scientific Data Systems to Xerox Data Systems.

Corporate egos aside, when should a company use the house name and when should they select a new name? (You can't really disregard corporate egos. Try telling General Electric not to put the GE name on a new product and you'll begin to appreciate the enormity of the corporate ego problem.)

One reason why the principles of name selection remain so elusive is the Charles Lindbergh syndrome.

If you get into the mind first, any name is going to work.

If you didn't get there first, then you are flirting with disaster if you don't select an appropriate name.

Divide and conquer

To illustrate the advantages of separate names rather than house names, compare the strategies of Procter & Gamble with those of Colgate-Palmolive.

You'll find many house names in the Colgate-Palmolive line. To name a few: Colgate toothpaste, Colgate toothbrushes, Palmolive Rapid Shave, Palmolive dishwashing liquid, Palmolive soap.

You won't find any house names in the Procter & Gamble lineup. Procter & Gamble carefully positions each product so that it occupies a unique niche in the mind. For example: Tide makes clothes "white." Cheer makes tham "whiter than white." And Bold makes them "bright."

With fewer brands Procter & Gamble does twice as much business and makes five times as much profit as Colgate-Palmolive.

While it's fashionable on Madison Avenue these days to pooh-pooh Procter & Gamble advertising, it's interesting to note that Procter & Gamble makes more money every year than all of America's 6000 advertising agencies combined.

A new product needs a new name

When a really new product comes along, it's almost always a mistake to hang a well-known name on it.

The reason is obvious. A well-known name got well known because it stood for something. It occupies a position in the prospect's mind. A really well-known name sits on the top rung of a sharply defined ladder.

The new product, if it's going to be successful, is going to require a new ladder. New ladder, new name. It's as simple as that.

Yet the pressures to go with the well-known name are enormous. "A well-known name has built-in acceptance. Our customers and prospects know us and our company, and they will be more likely to accept our new product if we have our name on it." The logic of line extension is overwhelming and sometimes very difficult to refute.

Yet history has destroyed this illusion.

Xerox spent almost a billion dollars for a profitable computer company with a perfectly good name, Scientific Data Systems. Then what did Xerox do? Of course, they changed the name of the company from Scientific Data Systems to Xerox Data Systems.

Why? Obviously because Xerox was the better and more widely known name. And not only better known, but Xerox had a marketing mystique. A corporate Cinderella, Xerox could do no wrong.

The teeter-totter principle

When you look into the prospect's mind, you can see what went wrong.

It's the teeter-totter principle. One name can't stand for two distinctly different products. When one goes up, the other goes down.

Xerox means copier, not computer. (If you asked your secretary to get you a Xerox copy, you'd be upset if you got a reel of mag tape.)

Even Xerox knew this. "This Xerox machine can't make a copy," said the headline of one of their computer ads.

You knew that any Xerox machine that couldn't make a copy was headed for trouble. When Xerox folded its computer operations, it wrote off an additional $84.4 million.

What's a Heinz? It used to mean pickles. Heinz owned the pickle position and got the largest share.

Then the company made Heinz mean ketchup. Very successfully too. Heinz is now the No. 1 brand of ketchup.

But what happened to the other side of the teeter-totter? Why, of course, Heinz lost its pickle leadership to Vlasic.

To be successful, Xerox would have had to make Xerox mean computers.

Does this make sense for a company like Xerox that owns the copier position? A company that gets most of its volume from copiers?

Xerox is more than a name. It's a position. Like Kleenex, Hertz, and Cadillac, Xerox represents a position of enormous long-term value.

It's bad enough when someone tries to take your position away. It's tragic when you do it to yourself.

Anonymity is a resource

One reason why companies keep looking for a free ride is that they underestimate the value of anonymity.

In politics, in marketing, in life, anonymity is a resource, easily squandered by too much publicity.

"You can't beat somebody with a nobody," goes the old political saying. But today you can.

The rapid rise of a "nobody" like Gary Hart is proof that politics is a different game today. The old maxims are no longer valid.

Richard Nixon may be the best-known political name in the world. But almost any nobody could beat him.

Publicity is like eating. Nothing kills the appetite quite as much as a hearty meal. And nothing kills the publicity potential of a product or a person quite as much as a cover story in a national magazine.

The media are constantly looking for the new and different, the fresh young face.

In dealing with media, you must conserve your anonymity until you are ready to spend it. And then when you spend it, spend it big. Always keeping in mind that the objective is not publicity or communication for its own sake, but publicity to achieve a position in the prospect's mind.

An unknown company with an unknown product has much more to gain from publicity than a well-known company with an established product.

"In the future everyone will be famous for 15 minutes," Andy Warhol once predicted.

When your 15 minutes arrive, make the most of every second.

12

The line-extension trap

When the marketing history of the past decade is written, the single most significant trend will have to be line extension. That is, taking the name of an established product and using it on a new one. (The free-ride trap carried to its ultimate conclusion.)

Dial soap, Dial deodorant.

Life Savers candy. Life Savers gum.

Kleenex tissue. Kleenex towels.

Line extension has swept through the advertising and marketing community like Sherman through Georgia. And for some very sound reasons.

Logic is on the side of line extension. Arguments of economics. Trade acceptance. Consumer acceptance. Lower advertising costs. Increased income. The corporate image.

Inside-out thinking

Logic is on the side of line extension. Truth, unfortunately, is not.

Line extension is a result of clear, hard-headed, inside-out thinking that goes something like this:

"We make Dial soap, a great product that gets the biggest share of the bar-soap market. When our customers see Dial deodorant, they'll know it comes from the makers of the great Dial soap."

"Furthermore," and this is the clincher, "Dial is a deodorant soap. Our customers will expect us to produce a high-quality underarm deodorant." In short, Dial soap customers will buy Dial deodorants.

Notice, however, how the rationale changes when the line extension is in the same category.

Bayer "invented" aspirin and marketed the leading brand of analgesic for many years. The people at Bayer couldn't fail to notice the progress made by the "anti-aspirin" approach used by Tylenol.

So Bayer introduced an acetaminophen product called "Bayer nonaspirin pain reliever." Presumably people who had been buying Tylenol and other acetaminophen products would now switch back to Bayer, the leading name in headache remedies.

But neither strategy worked.

Dial has a large share of the soap market and a very small share of the deodorant market.

And Bayer nonaspirin never got more than a tiny share of the acetaminophen market.

Outside-in thinking

Let's look at line extension from the point of view of the prospect and work backward.

Both Dial and Bayer hold strong positions inside the prospect's mind.

But what does it mean to own a position in the mind? Simply this: The brand name becomes a surrogate or substitute for the generic name.

"Where is the Bayer?"

"Hand me the Dial."

The stronger the position, the more often this substitution takes place. Some brands are so strong they are practically generic. Fiberglas, Formica, Jell-O, Kleenex, Band-Aid, Sanka.

"Generic" brand names are, of course, close to the edge, so they have to be handled carefully or Uncle Sam will take your goodies away.

From a communication point of view, the generic brand name is very efficient. One word serves in place of two. When you have a generic brand name, you can afford to ignore the brand and promote the category.

"Coffee keeps you awake? Drink Sanka."

"Serve your family low-calorie Jell-O instead of cake or pie."

From the prospect's point of view, line extension works against the generic brand position. It blurs the sharp focus of the brand in the mind. No longer can the prospect say "Bayer" if he or she wants aspirin. Or "Dial" for soap.

In a sense, line extension educates the prospect to the fact that Bayer is nothing but a brand name. It destroys the illusion that Bayer is a superior form of aspirin. Or that Dial is deodorant soap rather than just a brand name for a deodorant soap.

JCPenney vs. DieHard

What actually gets driven into the mind is not the product at all but the "name" of the product, which the prospect uses as a hook to hang attributes on.

So if the name of the automobile battery is the DieHard and Sears tells you that it will last 48 months, you have a hook (DieHard) to hang the long-lasting idea on.

But if the name of the battery is the JCPenney battery and the retailer tells you it never needs water, you have a very weak hook (JCPenney) to hang this feature on.

In a physical sense, the name is also like the point of a knife. It opens up the mind to let the message penetrate. With the right name, the product fills the creneau and stays there.

So why would JCPenney call it the JCPenney battery? Presumably there were other communicative words like DieHard available.

It's easy to see why if you apply "inside-out" thinking. "We're the JCPenney company. We're highly respected among all kinds of buyers including battery buyers. We'll put our own name on the product so that everyone will instantly know who made it and that it's an exceptionally good product."

Then the clincher. "With the JCPenney name on the battery, the prospect will know where to buy it."

"Terrific thinking, J. C." And another logical inside-out decision is made.

But when the tables are turned, the name makes no sense because the mind of the prospect is organized differently. The prospect thinks in terms of products.

It should come as no surprise that in terms of brand preference (the battery ladder in the mind of the prospect) the DieHard sits on the top rung and JCPenney is way down the line.

But doesn't a big retailer like JCPenney sell a lot of batteries? Of course, but as everyone knows, many products with the wrong name are sold "in spite of" rather than "because of."

On the other hand, doesn't the prospect have difficulty remembering that the DieHard battery can only be bought at Sears? Yes, it is a problem for Sears and not everyone who might want to buy the DieHard will be able to make the connection. But it's better to establish a position in the prospect's mind first and then worry about how to establish a retail connection later.

In positioning, the shortest distance between two points is not necessarily the best strategy. The obvious name isn't always the best name.

Inside-out thinking is the biggest barrier to success. Outside-in thinking is the best aid.

Two ways of looking at the name

The consumer and the manufacturer see things in totally different ways.

Would you believe that to the folks down in Atlanta, Coca-Cola is not a soft drink? To the manufacturer, Coca-Cola is a company, a brand name, an institution, and a great place to work.

But to the consumer, Coca-Cola is a sweet, dark, carbonated beverage. What's in the glass is Coke. It's not a cola drink manufactured by a company called Coca-Cola.

The tablets in a bottle of aspirin are Bayer. Not aspirin manufactured by a company called Bayer. (The company name, of course, is Sterling Drug, not Bayer. So Bayer nonaspirin could just as logically have been called Sterling nonaspirin.)

The great strength of a generic brand name is this close identification with the product itself. In the consumer's mind, Bayer is aspirin and every other aspirin brand becomes "imitation Bayer."

The Coca-Cola slogan, "The real thing," capitalizes on the tendency of the prospect to put the first product into the mind on a pedestal and to treat the me-too products as somehow inferior to the original.

If Coke or Kleenex or Bayer is not available or if other brands are cheap enough, then the prospect might buy something else. But Bayer would still own a strong position in the mind.

But notice what happens when the same customer is asked to buy a product called "Bayer nonaspirin." If Bayer is aspirin, how can Bayer also be nonaspirin?

Bayer timed-release aspirin, Bayer decongestant cold tablets, Bayer nonaspirin pain reliever. Each extension of the Bayer line undercuts the brand's aspirin position.

As you might expect, Bayer's total share of the analgesic market keeps falling.

What's a Protein 21?

Perhaps the classic example of the line-extension trap is what happened to Protein 21 shampoo.

A number of years ago the Mennen company introduced a combination shampoo/conditioner called Protein 21, which rapidly carved out a 13 percent share of the shampoo market.

Then Mennen hit the line-extension lure. In rapid succession, the company introduced Protein 21 hairspray in regular and extra hold, scented and unscented. Also Protein 21 conditioner (in two formulas) and Protein 21 concentrate. And to make sure you can't remember what to put on your hair, Mennen also markets Protein 29. For men.

No wonder Protein 21's share of the shampoo market has fallen from 13 percent to 2 percent. And the decline is bound to continue.

But as incredible as it may seem, line extensions continue to sweep the packaged goods field.

What's a Scott?

Take the position of Scott in paper products. Scott has the lion's share of the billion-dollar market for towels, napkins, toilet tissues, and other consumer paper products. But Scott was weak where they thought they were strong.

ScotTowels, ScotTissue, Scotties, Scotkins, even BabyScott diapers. All of these names undermine the Scott foundation. The more products hung on the Scott name, the less meaning the name has to the average consumer.

Take ScotTissue, for example. ScotTissue was the No. 1 brand in the toilet-tissue market. Then Mr. Whipple and his tissue squeezers at Procter & Gamble moved in. Now ScotTissue is second to Charmin.

In Scott's case, a large share of market didn't mean they owned the position. More important is a large share of mind. The consumer could write "Charmin, Kleenex, Bounty, and Pampers" on a shopping list and we'd know exactly what products he or she was going to get. "Scott" on a shopping list has no meaning.

The actual brand names aren't much help either. Which brand, for example, is engineered for the nose, Scotties or ScotTissue?

In positioning terms, the name Scott exists in limbo. It isn't firmly ensconced on any product ladder.

Scott has begun to see the error of its ways. Viva paper towels, a Scott brand, is a winner. So is Cottonelle bathroom tissue.

What's a Life Saver?

Life Savers gum is another example of line extension that went nowhere.

Again, the logic is on the side of line extension. In an article in *The New York Times,* Life Savers' executive vice president explained the strategy:

"I am convinced that one way to improve the odds is by transferring an existing strong name to a new product requiring similar attributes."

Then he explains the attributes of Life Savers candy: "Our consumer dialogue indicates that the Life Savers brand name conveys more than merely the candy with the hole. It also means excellence in flavor, outstanding value, and dependable quality."

Not exactly. How many people would have said "Life Savers" if you asked them, "What brand means excellence in flavor, outstanding value, and dependable quality?" None.

Now what if you ask them "What's the name of the candy with the hole?"

Most people would say "Life Savers."

So what happened to Life Savers gum? The product never got more than a few percent of the market. One of those brands you won't see anymore because it was quietly killed.

As the television commercials used to say, "It's a great product, but where's the hole?"

The hole, of course, is not in the product at all. It's in the marketing strategy.

Ironically, Life Savers, Inc. has a big success in the gum field. The bubble gum field.

No, it wasn't Life Savers bubble gum.

It's Bubble Yum. The first brand of soft bubble gum. (The advantage of being first plus the advantage of not using a line-extension name.)

Bubble Yum is a runaway success. Sales already exceed those of Life Savers candy.

Not only is Bubble Yum the largest-selling brand of bubble gum, it's likely to become the largest-selling brand of chewing gum of any type.

What's an Eveready?

Many companies find themselves in rough water when new technologies rock their boats.

Eveready, a product of Union Carbide, dominated the battery market when flashlights were the principal application. Then came the transistor and with it a host of new products including tape recorders and more powerful radios. And, of course, the longer-lasting alkaline batteries.

P. R. Mallory saw the opportunity and introduced the Duracell alkaline battery in a distinctive black and gold case.

The folks at Union Carbide pooh-poohed the idea of a new name. "We've already got the best name in the battery business," they said.

But to hedge their bets, the Union Carbide people copied the Duracell black and gold color scheme. And gave the words "alkaline power cell" more prominence than the Eveready trademark.

The Duracell battery just says Duracell in bold type. It doesn't need to say "alkaline power cell" because Duracell means alkaline power cell.

This, of course, is the essence of positioning. To make your brand name stand for the generic. So the prospect freely uses the brand name for the generic.

Finally the Union Carbide people gave up and decided to copy the Duracell approach. The Eveready alkaline power cell became the Energizer which finally is giving Duracell a run for its money.

Line extension seems so intuitively right that company after company falls into the trap. Examples are not hard to find. They're a saga of opportunities missed.

The 100-mm dud

What's the name of the first extra-long, 100-mm cigarette?

Benson & Hedges, right? It's the best-known and largest-selling 100-mm brand.

"The disadvantages of Benson & Hedges" launched the brand and burned the name into the mind of the cigarette smokers.

Benson & Hedges became known as the first, the original, the inventor of the 100-mm concept.

But, of course, it wasn't. The first 100-mm cigarette was Pall Mall Gold, but Pall Mall fell into the line-extension trap.

Then Benson & Hedges moved in and preempted the long-cigarette position.

You'd think the missed opportunity represented by Pall Mall Gold would have discouraged them.

But it didn't. As we said, the logic in favor of line extension is overwhelming.

So now we have Pall Mall Menthol, Pall Mall Extra Mild, and Pall Mall Light 100s. The confusion has detracted from sales of the basic Pall Mall brand.

Take Pall Mall Menthol, for example. Again, the logic is unassailable to the manufacturer. "Menthol cigarettes like Kool and Salem are getting a larger and larger share of the market. . . . If we had a menthol brand, we could capture a share of that growing market."

Introducing Pall Mall Menthol. Which never achieved more than 7 percent of the volume of Kool.

In 1964 Pall Mall was the No. 1 cigarette brand in the United States.

In 1965 Pall Mall line-extended for the first time. They also fell to second place in sales. Every year since, Pall Mall's share of the American cigarette market has declined.

From 14.4 percent in 1964 to 3.8 percent today.

Line-extension logic in cigarettes should work two ways. Since regular brands represent a large share of the market, would you introduce a Kool nonmenthol?

Of course not. Kool was the original menthol cigarette. Kool means menthol. Like Bayer means aspirin.

Today a well-stocked tobacco shop will carry well over 100 different brands (including line extensions) out of an industry that produces in the neighborhood of 175 brands. It boggles the mind.

Naturally, the two leading brands, Marlboro and Winston, have long since line-extended the lights, 100-mm, and menthol. So according to the theory, can you expect to see the Marlboro and Winston brands follow in Pall Mall's steps? Perhaps. But in the land of the blind, the one-eyed man is king.

What brands are left to challenge the leaders? Almost all major cigarette brands have been line-extended to death.

Confusion in corn oils

What's the name of the first corn-oil margarine?

Fleischmann's is the leading brand of corn-oil margarine and the biggest seller.

But the first corn-oil margarine was Mazola. A classic example of logic leading you astray.

Mazola was the name of the leading brand of liquid corn oil. What more logical choice for a corn-oil margarine than Mazola? Mazola corn oil. Mazola corn-oil margarine. And the rest is history.

Fleischmann's is the No. 1 brand today.

Oddly enough, Fleischmann's margarine, if you want to get technical, is a line-extended name. Remember Fleischmann's yeast? Fortunately for Fleischmann's, few people do because few people bake their own bread today.

And then there is Fleischmann's gin, vodka, and whisky, also from the same company. The confusion factor is minimized because of the mental distance between a liquor product and a margarine. (Who really believes that Cadillac dog food is made by General Motors?)

The coffee-cup caper

Another missed opportunity took place in the freeze-dried coffee field. Today Taster's Choice is the leading brand and the largest seller.

But what was the name of the first freeze-dried coffee? Maxim. So why isn't Maxim the No. 1 brand? It's a story of intrigue and courage that might be worth telling in more detail.

With its Maxwell House brand, General Foods owned the coffee market. The company got the largest share and made the most money. Then it invented a new process called "freeze-dried instant."

On the surface this seemed to be a way for General Foods to increase its share of the coffee market.

Or was it?

General Foods' opening move was good news for competition. By using the name Maxim, a spinoff of the Maxwell House name, the company instantly became vulnerable. (Maxim, Maxwell, get it? Most people didn't.) Maxim is a meaningless word that doesn't connote a benefit.

The Nestlé counterattack was named Taster's Choice. Not only was the strategic choice of the name superb, but Nestlé's advertising was just about perfect.

"Tastes like ground roast," said the Taster's Choice ads, relating the freeze-dried coffee brand to the standard of excellence, ground-roasted coffee.

Taster's Choice is the big winner in the coffee-cup caper. In spite of the fact that General Foods invented the freeze-dried category and was first on the scene, Taster's Choice outsells Maxim 2 to 1.

The fickle-fingers affair

Another missed opportunity is known in hand lotion circles as "the fickle-fingers affair." The story starts with Jergens, the No. 1 brand with the dominant share of market.

First, the company introduced Jergens Extra Dry, a cream-like product in an era of liquidlike lotions. Jergens Extra Dry was really a significant innovation smothered by the similarity of names. The prospect didn't recognize the difference.

But the competition did.

Chesebrough-Pond's introduced Intensive Care. Now for the first time, the new creamlike lotion had a name which positioned the product clearly in the consumer's mind. And the product took off.

Of course, when Jergens realized what was happening, they countered with a brand called Direct Aid.

But it was the old story of too little and too late because the marketing victory went to Intensive Care. Today Intensive Care is the No. 1 brand. It outsells Jergens, Jergens Extra Dry, and Direct Aid combined.

But isn't the brand really called "Vaseline Intensive Care," a line-extended name?

True, but customers call the product Intensive Care, not Vaseline. In the mind of the prospect Vaseline is petroleum jelly; Intensive Care is a hand lotion.

Reverse line extension

While line extension is usually a mistake, the reverse can work. Reverse line extension is called "broadening the base." One of the best examples is Johnson's baby shampoo.

By promoting the mildness of the product to the adult market, the company has made Johnson's baby shampoo one of the leading brands of adult shampoo.

Notice the characteristics of this broadening-the-base strategy. Same product, same package, same label. Only the application has changed.

If Johnson & Johnson had line-extended the product and introduced Johnson's adult shampoo, the product would not have been nearly as successful.

Another example of broadening the base is Blue Nun, a white wine being promoted as equally good with meat courses as with fish.

But aren't these examples of the "everybody trap"? Not exactly. Johnson's baby shampoo is the first and only baby shampoo being promoted as an adult product too. And Blue Nun is the only white wine being advertised as good with meat as well as fish.

If other brands tried the same approach, they wouldn't be nearly as successful as these two.

And then there is Arm & Hammer baking soda, being promoted as good for refrigerators and drains. Very successfully too. But what happened when the same company line-extended with Arm & Hammer, the baking soda deodorant?

Very little. As Phyllis Diller says, "It only works if you're standing in the refrigerator."

13

When line extension can work

Line extension is popular. No doubt about it.

At one point in time, professional baseball, football, basketball, and tennis teams in the New York City area were known as the Mets, Jets, Nets, and Sets.

The city's off-track betting offices put up posters featuring the New York Bets. If the city had a gym team, presumably they would be called the New York Sweats.

Why stop there? A street gang could be the New York Ghetts. City planners, the New York Debts.

Fortunately for one's sanity, the trend seems to be in the other direction. The tennis team changed its name from the New York Sets to the New York Apples.

Short-term advantages

One of the reasons for the continuing popularity of line extension is that in the short term, line extension has some advantages.

Let's say there was going to be a professional swimming team in New York. "Here come the Wets" might be a typical newspaper headline announcing the event. With one word, "Wets," we know it's (1) a professional sports team, (2) located in the metropolitan New York area, and (3) involved in some kind of water sport.

But that's only in the short term. As the original announcement fades in the mind, confusion sets in.

Is there really a swimming team called the Wets? Or have I confused them with a basketball team called the Nets? Or was I thinking about a tennis team called the Sets? Now let's see, the Nets changed their name to the Apples. Or was it the Sets that changed their name to the Apples?

Because the line-extension name is related to the original name, it achieves an instant flash of understanding. "Ah, yes, Diet Coca-Cola."

It also generates an instant flash of sales. When Alka-Seltzer announces a new product like Alka-Seltzer Plus, everybody stocks up on it. Consumers aren't necessarily buying it, but retailers are.

So the early sales figures look good. (To book $1 million worth of business, you only have to sell $35 worth to every supermarket.)

Business looks great the first 6 months as you fill the pipelines. But when the reorders don't come in, all of a sudden things turn dark.

Long-term disadvantages

After the initial recognition of a line-extension brand, the prospect is never quite sure there is such a product.

Schlitz Light, Pall Mall Extra Mild, Jergens Extra Dry. Brand names like these slide into (and out of) the mind effortlessly. They require almost no mental work on the part of the prospect.

Easy come, easy go. Line-extension names are forgettable because they have no independent position in the mind. They are satellites to the original brand name. Their only contribution is to blur the position occupied by the original name. Often with catastrophic results.

Way back in the thirties, the Ralston Purina Company was running radio commercials for "Ralston 1, 2, 3." One was Shredded Ralston. Two was Regular Ralston. Three was Instant Ralston.

One, two, three, they're all gone.

And the legendary David Ogilvy broke his pencil writing advertisements combining Rinso White with Rinso Blue.

Sara Lee tried to get into the frozen dinner field with products like Sara Lee Chicken & Noodles Au Gratin and Sara Lee Beef & Pepper Stew.

Sara Lee owns the dessert position. Nobody doesn't like Sara Lee, but there were a lot of people out there who didn't like the chicken & noodles au gratin. And didn't buy it. Especially with the name Sara Lee on it.

So the kitchens of Sara Lee came in out of the frozen entree field. After dropping some $8 million on the project.

Almost everybody has tried line extension. *Saturday Review Magazine* tried to publish in four different flavors—*The Arts, Science, Education, The Society*. A $17 million loss.

Levi Strauss and Brown Shoe tried to launch, would you believe, "Levi's for Feet." Levi is, by far, the market leader in jeans, but this time they booted it.

Then there is Avis flowers, Zenith watches, Old Grand-Dad tobacco, Bic pantyhose, Kleenex diapers.

Also Pierre Cardin wine. In both red and white, of course. And Chanel for Men.

"Two" seems to be a popular line-extension concept. We have Alka-2, Dial 2, Sominex 2, as well as Jaws 2. (Almost never has a motion picture sequel generated as much business as the original.)

Even advertising agencies have jumped into twos. Ogilvy & Mather 2, Doyle Dane Bernbach 2, N. W. Ayer 2, and Grey 2, to name a few twos.

But the most shocking announcement of all came from Procter & Gamble. After decades of resisting the line-extension fad, P&G spend $50 million to introduce Liquid Tide. "We expect Liquid Tide to be the No. 1 liquid," said a P&G spokesperson.

But Liquid Tide is unlikely to topple the industry leader, Wisk. Furthermore, the new product is sure to cannibalize Tide powder.

The shopping-list test

The classic test for line extension is the shopping list.

Just list the brands you want to buy on a piece of paper and send your spouse to the supermarket: Kleenex, Bayer, and Dial.

That's easy enough. Most husbands or wives would come back with Kleenex tissue, Bayer aspirin, and Dial soap.

Line extensions like Kleenex towels, Bayer non-aspirin, and Dial antiperspirants have not destroyed the brands' original positions. Yet. But give them enough time to hang themselves.

How about this list: Heinz, Scott, Kraft.

Will your spouse bring back Heinz pickles or ketchup (or perhaps baby food)? Scott tissue or towels? Kraft cheese, mayonnaise, or salad dressing?

The confusion caused when one name stands for more than one product is slowly but surely sapping the strength of brands like Scott and Kraft.

Like a star that's overexpanded, the brand eventually becomes a burned-out hulk. An enormous marketing white elephant. What makes line extension so insidious is that the disease takes many years to exact its toll. Many years of slow, debilitating existence.

Take Kraft. A famous name which suffers from terminal line extension.

What's a Kraft? It's everything and yet it's nothing. In almost no categories is the Kraft brand number one. In mayonnaise, Kraft is second to Hellmann's. In salad dressing, Kraft is second to Wishbone.

Where Kraftco has the leading brand in a category, they don't call it Kraft.

In cream cheese, it's Philadelphia, not Kraft.

In ice cream, it's Sealtest, not Kraft.

In margarine, it's Parkay, not Kraft.

Where is the strength of the Kraft name? It's too diffuse. Kraft means everything and nothing. Line extension is a weakness, not a strength.

What about cheese? Surely Kraft is a strong name in cheese. And it is.

"America," say the ads, "spells cheese K-R-A-F-T." Terrible spelling and terrible strategy.

Marketing is like horse racing. The winning horse is not necessarily a good horse. It all depends on the ability of the horses in the race. In a claiming race, the winner is the best of the worst. In a stakes race, the best is the best.

Kraft has been successful in cheese. Now, name all the other cheese brands you known.

Kraft is a winner in a claiming race.

Where there are no brands or weak brands, you can line-extend. But as soon as strong competition arrives, you're in trouble.

The bartender test

In addition to the shopping list test, there's the bartender test. What do you get when you order the brand by name?

"J&B on the rocks" should get you scotch. "A Beefeater martini" should arrive with gin. And "a bottle of Dom Perignon" will definitely get you champagne.

What about "Cutty on the rocks"? You'll get scotch, of course, but will you get Cutty Sark or the more expensive 12-year-old Cutty 12?

Cutty 12 is a typical example of twisted thinking. Combine a well-known name (Cutty) with a descriptive adjective (12). Very logical from the point of view of the distillery. But what about the point of view of the drinker?

When you order "Chivas on the rocks," you let everyone know you want the best. Chivas Regal.

To get Cutty 12, you can't just say "Cutty." And when you add the "12," you're never quite sure whether the bartender heard you or, just as important, whether the people around you heard the "12."

Nor does the promotion of Cutty 12 help the original Cutty Sark brand. It's a constant reminder to the Cutty Sark drinker that he or she is drinking a lower-quality product.

Cutty 12 got into the ball game after Chivas Regal, so we shouldn't have expected much. But there was a 12-year-old brand of scotch in the U.S. market well before Chivas.

Johnnie Walker Black Label.

Today, of course, Chivas Regal outsells Johnnie Walker Black Label by a considerable margin.

"Give me a Johnnie Walker with a splash, bartender."

"Black Label or Red Label, sir?"

"Aaaaaaaaaaaah . . . the hell with it. Make it a Chivas."

Cutty 12 and Johnnie Walker Black Label are step-up examples of line extension. They usually result in anemic sales at the higher-priced end. (Who wants to pay premium prices for a low-price name?)

What's a Packard?

The step-down problem is just the reverse. Step-down products are often instantly successful. The hangover comes later.

Before World War II Packard was the premier American automobile. More so even than Cadillac, it was a status symbol esteemed all over the world.

Heads of state bought armored Packards. One was made for Franklin Roosevelt. Like Rolls-Royce, Packard loftily declined the annual model-change policy of lesser makers. They positioned themselves above the pack.

Then in the middle thirties, Packard introduced their first step-down model, the relatively inexpensive Packard Clipper.

The Packard Clipper was the most successful car Packard ever built. Sales were terrific, but it killed the company. (Or more precisely, it killed Packard's prestige position, which in turn killed the company.)

Packard drifted along until 1954 when Studebaker absorbed the company. The end of the road came years later.

What's a Cadillac?

What do you know about Cadillac? How long is it? What colors does it come in? What's the horsepower of the engine? What options are available?

To the average automobile prospect, General Motors has succeeded in communicating almost nothing about Cadillac. Except its position as the top-of-the-line, domestic luxury automobile.

But even General Motors sometimes forgets that for every product there are two points of view. And most line-extension mistakes are made because the marketer did not appreciate this fact.

What's a Cadillac? This might surprise you, but from General Motors' point of view, a Cadillac is not an automobile at all. It's a division. As a matter of fact, it's one of GM's most profitable divisions.

But from the buyer's point of veiw, Cadillac is a big luxury car. You can see the problem.

Because of the gasoline situation, Cadillac is worried. So to maintain that profitability, General Motors has introduced a small Cadillac, the Cimarron. But in the long-term a mini-Cadillac conflicts with the big-car position that Cadillac owns in the mind.

So the prospect looks at the Cimarron and asks, "Is it or isn't it a Cadillac?"

Long-term, the Cimarron gets in the way of the most effective answer to the challenge of smaller luxury cars like Mercedes and BMW. To establish a small luxury brand, General Motors needs a separate high-price name and a separate dealer organization.

What's a Chevrolet?

For automobiles as well as other products, you can ask yourself that age-old question and you'll know if you have a positioning problem.

What is it?

For example, what's a Chevrolet? It's a car that's fallen into the everybody trap. By trying to appeal to everybody, a product winds up appealing to nobody.

What's a Chevrolet? We'll tell you what a Chevrolet is. It's a big, small, cheap, expensive car.

O.K., how come Chevy is still No. 1? How come they haven't lost their leadership to Ford?

To which we reply, "What's a Ford?" Same problem. Ford is also a big, small, cheap, expensive car.

Ford has another problem. Not only is Ford an automobile brand. Ford is also a company.

A Ford Ford might be all right, but there is a real problem for the company in selling Ford Mercurys or Ford Lincolns. (One reason why the Ford Motor Company has always had a hard time selling higher-priced cars.)

What's a Volkswagen?

A line-extension tragedy usually moves to its inevitable conclusion in three acts.

Act One is the big success, the big breakthrough. Usually the result of finding a wide-open creneau and then exploiting it brilliantly.

Volkswagen invented the small-car position and moved rapidly to exploit the breakthrough. "Think small," perhaps the most famous single advertisement every run, stated the position in no uncertain terms.

Very quickly, the Volkswagen Beetle established an exceptionally strong position in the automotive market. Like most classic success stories, Volkswagen became more than a brand name for a product.

"I drive a Volkswagen" says more than who made the automobile the person owns. "I drive a Volkswagen" says something about the owner's way of life. A no-nonsense, practical person, self-confident about his or her status in life. A simple, functional piece of transportation equipment.

The Volkswagen owner is a reverse snob. He or she loves to put down the car buyer who loves to impress the neighbors. "The 1970 Volkswagen will stay ugly longer" expresses this attitude perfectly.

Act Two is fueled by greed and visions of unending successes. So Volkswagen extends Volkswagen reliability and quality to bigger, more expensive cars. To buses and jeep-type vehicles.

Act Three is the denouement. Is it possible that eight models won't sell as well as one? It's not only possible, it happened.

From first place in imported cars, Volkswagen fell to fourth. Behind Toyota, Datson, and Honda. And just barely ahead of Mazda and Subaru.

The pattern of early success followed by line extension followed by disillusionment is fairly common. After all, you can't expect companies like Scott and Volkswagen to rest on their laurels. You'd expect them to find new fields to conquer. So how do they go about finding them? One way is obvious. They develop a new concept or a new product with a new position and a new name to match.

A name is a rubber band

It will stretch, but not beyond a certain point. Furthermore, the more you stretch a name, the weaker it becomes. (Just the opposite of what you might expect.)

How far should you stretch a name? This is an economics call as much as a judgment call.

Let's say you have a line of canned vegetables. Do you have a brand name for peas, another for corn, and still a third for string beans? Probably not. Economically, it wouldn't make sense.

So Del Monte is probably right to use the same brand name on its line of canned fruits and vegetables. But notice what happens when a competitor zeroes in on a single product. The Dole line of canned pineapple.

Dole vs. Del Monte in pineapple is no contest. Dole wins every time.

So what does Dole do next? It puts the Dole name on fresh bananas. The Dole banana.

Let's say Dole is successful in making Dole mean bananas. So what happens to pineapple? It's the teeter-totter principle with bananas on one side and pineapple on the other.

But can't Dole do what Del Monte did? Become a full-line supplier of canned and fresh food products?

Sure, but only at the expense of sacrificing its valuable pineapple franchise. And with the added disadvantage of being the last to line-extend.

Rules of the road

We call line extension a "trap," not a mistake. Line extension can work if. . . .

But it's a big if. If your competitors are foolish. If your volumn is small. If you have no competitors. If you don't expect to build a position in the prospect's mind. If you don't do any advertising.

The truth is, many products are sold, few are positioned.

That is, the customer will pick up a can of peas without having a going-in preference, or position, for a brand of peas. In this case, any well-known brand name is going to do better than any unknown name.

And if you work for a company with thousands of small-volume products (3M is a typical example), you obviously cannot have a new name for every one.

So we offer some rules of the road that will tell you when to use the house name and when not to.

1. **Expected volume.** Potential winners should not bear the house name. Small-volume products should.

2. **Competition.** In a vacuum, the brand should not bear the house name. In a crowded field, it should.

3. **Advertising support.** Big-budget brands should not bear the house name. Small-budget brands should.

4. **Significance.** Breakthrough products should not bear the house name. Commodity products such as chemicals should.

5. **Distribution.** Off-the-shelf items should not bear the house name. Items sold by sales reps should.

14 Positioning a company: Xerox

You can position anything. A person, a product, a politician. Even a company.

Why would anyone want to position a company? Who buys a company? And why would a company want to sell itself? To whom? (To protect themselves against unfriendly takeovers, most companies would like to be invisible.)

The buying and selling of companies

Actually, a lot of buying and selling of companies is going on. Only it's called different names.

When a new employee accepts a job, he or she "buys" the company. (With its recruiting programs, a company is actually selling itself.)

Who would you rather work for, General Electric or the Schenectady Electrical Works?

Every year companies across the country compete for top graduates at the nation's leading universities. Who do you think gets the cream of the crop?

That's right. The companies that occupy the best positions in the minds of the prospective employee. The General Electrics, the Procter & Gambles.

And when investors buy a share of stock, what they are really paying for is a piece of that company's position, now and in the future.

How much a person is willing to pay for that stock (six or sixty times earnings) depends on the strength of that position in the buyer's mind.

Positioning a company effectively has lots of advantages if you happen to be an officer or director of that corporation. It's not easy, though.

The name problem again

First of all, the name. Especially the name. Would you believe that Pullman doesn't happen to be much of a factor in the railroad car business anymore?

And that bus revenues represent only a small part of Greyhound's total sales.

Both Pullman and Greyhound have changed drastically. Yet the way they are perceived by the public has scarcely changed at all. Their names have locked them to their past reputations.

Yet they have tried. Especially Greyhound, which has spent millions of dollars telling the financial community that it is "more than a bus company."

But as long as those buses with the long slim dogs on the side go zipping up and down the interstate highways, the corporate advertising is an expensive mistake. If Greyhound wants to be more than a bus company, it needs a new name. A "more than a bus company" name.

But even with the right name, the corporate positioning job isn't done. Your company's name ought to stand for something within your industry.

Standing for something

Consider Ford. Everyone knows that Ford is an automobile company. But what kind of car is a Ford?

Ford can't build a corporate position on a specific kind of car, because it builds them in all types and all sizes, including trucks. (Whether it should or not is another matter.)

So the positioning question boils down to some quality to be found across the board in all vehicles.

The company has settled on "innovation" as the key attribute in a vehicle from Ford. Result: the "Ford has a better idea" campaign.

Not bad, but many corporate programs settle on a mundane and hackneyed approach. Of which the most mundane and hackneyed, perhaps, is one based on people.

"Our people are our greatest resource."

"Gulf people: Meeting the challenge."

"Grumman: We're proud of the many products we make. We're prouder of the people who make them."

Are there no differences in quality between the people in one company and those in another?

Of course there are. But it's quite another matter to build a position based on better people.

Most people think that the bigger, more successful companies have the better people. And the smaller, less successful companies have the leftovers.

So if your company occupies the top rung of the product ladder in the prospect's mind, you can be sure that the prospect will also think that your company has the best people.

If you're not on top and you tell the prospect you have the better people. . . . Well, that's one of those inconsistencies that doesn't usually get resolved in your favor.

If Ford really has the better ideas, why doesn't it use them in the marketplace to overtake General Motors instead of using them in its advertising to impress the public?

This is not a question of fact. (Ford could have the better ideas and still be in second place.) This is just a question that springs up in the prospect's mind.

And your advertising, to be successful, must answer this question.

Diversification is not the answer

Next to "people," the most common corporate positioning theme is "diversification." Companies want to become known as diversified manufacturers of a wide range of high-quality products.

But diversification is not effective as a corporate advertising approach. As a matter of fact, the two concepts of positioning and diversification are poles apart.

It's a fact of life that strong positions in the prospect's mind are built on major achievements. Not on broad product lines.

General Electric is known as the world's largest electrical manufacturer. Not as a diversified maker of industrial, transportation, chemical, and appliance products.

Even through General Electric makes thousands of consumer and industrial products, most of its successful products have been electrical ones. Most of its unsuccessful ones have been nonelectrical products. Computers being a typical example.

General Motors is known as the world's largest builder of automobiles. Not as a diversified maker of industrial, transportation, and appliance products.

IBM has a reputation as the world's largest computer manufacturer. Not as a worldwide manufacturer of many types of office machines.

A company may be able to make more money by diversifying. It should think twice, however, about trying to build a position based on that concept.

Even the stock market consistently undervalues conglomerates like ITT and Gulf & Western. (Many companies are worth more broken into parts than they are worth whole.)

Sometimes companies think they are concentrating their communication efforts when they are really not. The positioning concept becomes so broad that it is almost meaningless.

Which company used to call itself "a developer and supplier of information systems for work, education, and entertainment?"

Would you believe Bell & Howell? That's right, Bell & Howell.

How do you develop an effective position for a company? Let's look at Xerox, a company that seems to already have a position.

What's in Xerox's mind?

Why would Xerox want a position? Xerox has a position. Xerox is the Coca-Cola of copiers.

Quick, name another copier company? Nothing jumps into the mind, does it? Sure, after a while, you probably can remember that Sharp, Savin, Ricoh, Royal, and Canon make copiers. Even IBM and Kodak make copiers.

But nobody owns the copier position the way Xerox does. This is an enormous advantage in selling copiers. When you think your company needs another copier, your first thought is Xerox and your first telephone call is most likely to Xerox.

So what's the problem? Xerox sees the office market moving toward systems, expecially computer-based information systems. So Xerox bought Scientific Data Systems and subsequently changed the name to Xerox Data Systems.

"Our objective in acquiring SDS," said the chairman, "was to offer broader-based information systems. We feel that to really seize the opportunities around the world for supplying information, we had to broaden out from graphics, as IBM is broadening out into graphics. People in the seventies who can say to a customer, 'We can handle all your information needs, whether fascimile transmission, graphics, or whatever,' will have an enormous advantage."

Six years later, Xerox Data Systems folded. But the loss of XDS didn't stop Xerox from trying to broaden the company's product line. Xerox was still committed to the concept of going beyond copiers.

In the years to come, Xerox introduced a parade of office automation products. The XTEN network, the Ethernet network, the Star workstation, the 820 personal computer. "Now the industry will know our secret for certain," declared a Xerox vice president. "We want to be No. 1 in this market."

What's in the prospect's mind?

If Xerox would look into the minds of its prospects, it would quickly see that moving into office information systems is not in the cards.

The trade publication *Information Week* recently surveyed a sample of its subscribers. (The magazine has 100,000 subscribers, 80 percent of whom represent companies with 1000 or more employees. It would seem that this is the heart of the office automation market.)

Here are the answers given when subscribers were asked, "Which manufacturers of office information systems are you most interested in?"

IBM	81%
Wang	40%
Digital Equipment	36%
AT&T	22%
Hewlett-Packard	21%

Xerox didn't make the charts.

What can Xerox do? Our message to Xerox is to stop fighting copiers. You can't change what's in the prospect's mind.

Start using copiers. They could be your strongest asset. An asset in a strategic war with IBM and AT&T.

The "third-leg" strategy

It's a way for Xerox to take advantage of its heritage. As with many strategies, it's helpful to step back and get a sense of what has been going on in the marketplace.

Let's look first at the office of the past. Things were simple then. To put yourself in business, you got a telephone from AT&T, a typewriter from IBM, and a copier from Xerox.

Now look at the office of the present. All the action has been in the typewriter leg. Typewriters have been supplanted by computers. The telephone and copier legs have hardly changed at all.

What about the office of the future? If you believe everything you read, the office of the future will have a single leg consisting of an office automation system supplied by a single vendor. IBM, of course, is everyone's bet.

As a result, every manufacturer worth its computer is chasing this "single vendor" idea.

But systems don't always sell. The high-fidelity audio system was never supplied by one vendor as consumers picked the receivers and turntables and tape players they wanted.

The same went for the home entertainment center and the dream that GE had to sell all the major appliances in the kitchen. The woman of the house picked her favorite brands.

Furthermore, even if the office of the future should turn out to be one big system supplied by one big manufacturer, it's unlikely that Xerox would be a major factor.

Therefore, Xerox has nothing to lose and everything to gain by betting on a different scenario.

The "third-leg" scenario is a different view of the office of the future. It's a view that sees the office of the future as still having three legs. The telephone leg of AT&T becomes a communication leg with the addition of voice mail and facsimile equipment.

The typewriter leg of IBM becomes an input or processing leg with the addition of computers, workstations, and networks.

The question is what will Xerox add to the copier leg?

Some "cross-leg" difficulties

There's a good deal of evidence that the merging of legs is not the way of the future. History points to the difficulty of many "cross-leg" activities.

Take Xerox vs. IBM. (1) Xerox has not been very successful with computers, workstations, or local area networks, all of which belong to the leg owned by IBM. (2) On the other hand, IBM has not been very successful with copiers, a leg, or position, owned by Xerox.

Take Xerox vs. AT&T. (1) Nobody, including Xerox, has done very well with facsimile equipment, a leg owned by AT&T. (2) Voice mail and facsimile will take off as soon as AT&T gets behind them.

Take AT&T vs. IBM. (1) AT&T won't do well with computers, a leg owned by IBM. (2) On the other hand, IBM and Rolm won't do very well with telephones, a leg owned by AT&T. (Satellite Business Systems is losing $100 million a year.)

Even since Scientific Data Systems, Xerox has been trying to bridge the copier/computer gap. Instead of being an obstacle, the copier/computer gap in the long run could turn out to be Xerox's strongest ally.

"Third-leg" opportunities

If AT&T's telephone leg has become the communication leg and IBM's typewriter leg has become the input and processing leg, then what has Xerox's copier leg become?

The obvious answer is the output leg. There are many "third-leg" opportunities for Xerox as offices add computer printers, scanners, and storage devices to complement their copiers.

Furthermore, a hot new technology is moving into the output side of the office. That technology is the laser. There are laser printers, laser typesetters, laser memory systems.

Furthermore, the laser is making a name for itself in many other places. In communication, the laser is beginning to replace satellites. In the hospital, the laser is revolutionizing heart surgery. In the supermarket, you find laser check-out counters.

McDonnell/Douglas talks about a laser that is "capable of transmitting the entire contents of a 24-volume set of encyclopedia in a single second." United Telecom is setting up a nationwide laser network. AT&T is laying down a transatlantic laser link. GTE is bouncing laser beams off the moon.

In the consumer field, there is the laser videodisk player. The laser audiodisk player. And the laser everything disk which can play both video and audio.

No self-respecting rock show would end without a laser light show. Even Ronald Reagan's "star wars" satellites would be equipped with nuclear-powered laser weapons.

The fourth technology

In the past 30 years, three technologies have roared through the office and into the dictionary. The first was *thermography* by 3M, a photocopying process that uses infrared rays to produce a copy on a special type of paper.

The second was *xerography* by Xerox, a copying process that uses the action of light to produce a copy on plain paper.

The third is the *microprocessor* technology that computer companies like IBM have dominated.

There's an opportunity for Xerox to put another technological word in a yet to be published edition of Webster's Dictionary.

The fourth technology would be called "lasography." It could be defined as the process of communicating, printing, scanning, and storing optical or printed messages with the use of laser beams and optical fibers.

One word can say a lot

Xerox is a $9 billion company with more than 100,000 employees. It ought to be impossible to position an enterprise as big and diverse as Xerox with a single word.

But in an overcommunicated society there is only so much room in the mind. Today Xerox means just one word—copiers. Tomorrow Xerox could use lasography to create a broader mental position.

Lasography says new and different, and the business world loves things that are new and different.

Lasography sounds like a basic technology somehow related to xerography. In other words, it connects with Xerox's last big technology.

Lasography from Xerox, the company that's perceived to be in the "ography" business.

Lasography uses lasers, which are perceived to be on the leading edge of technology.

Lasography is the one concept that takes advantage of Xerox's position and broadens it to include the next generation of products.

In the positioning game you can't sit still. You must constantly be alert to keep your position targeted to today's problems and today's markets.

15 Positioning a country: Belgium

With the advent of relatively inexpensive airfare, we're fast becoming a world of tourists.

In days gone by, international travel was limited to the older, more affluent person. Today that's all changed. There was a time when the flight attendants were young and the travelers old. Now the travelers are young and the flight attendants are old.

The Sabena situation

One of the many North Atlantic carriers jockeying for these international travelers is an airline called Sabena Belgian World Airlines. But all competitors don't compete on an equal basis. TWA and Pan Am, for example, have for some time had a long list of gateway cities in both the United States and Europe.

But Sabena flies nonstop from North America to only one city in Europe: Brussels. Unless there was a hijacker aboard, every Sabena plane was going to land in Belgium.

While Sabena captured the lion's share of the traffic to Belgium, they were on a very meager diet. Not too many people were flying to this little country. Only one out of 50 North Atlantic passengers fly to Belgium.

On the country ladder in the prospective traveler's mind, Belgium was on one of the bottom rungs. If it was on the ladder at all.

One look at the situation and it was easy to tell what was wrong with Sabena's advertising. Sabena was using classic airline strategy. Sell the food and the service.

"Do I have to be a bon vivant to fly Sabena?" said a typical ad. But all the terrific food in the world won't induce you to fly an airline that isn't going where you want to go.

Position the country, not the airline

Sabena's most productive strategy was obviously not to position the airline but to position the country. In other words, do what KLM had done for Amsterdam.

Sabena had to make Belgium a place where a traveler would want to spend some time. Not a place you traveled through to get to somewhere else.

Furthermore, there's a moral here that shines through loud and clear. Whether you're selling colas, companies, or countries. Out of mind, out of business.

Most Americans knew very little about Belgium. They thought Waterloo was a suburb of Paris and the most important product of Belgium was waffles. Many didn't even know where the country was.

"If it's Tuesday, this must be Belgium," was the title of a popular motion picture.

But how do you find a position for a country? Well, if you think about it, the most successful countries all have strong mental images.

Say "England" and people think of pageantry, Big Ben, and the Tower of London.

Say "Italy" and they think of the Coliseum and St. Peter's and works of art.

Say "Amsterdam" and it's tulips, Rembrandt, and those wonderful canals.

Say "France" and it's food and the Eiffel Tower and the dazzling Riviera.

Your mind sees cities and countries as mental picture postcards. In your mind, New York is probably a skyline of tall buildings. San Francisco is cable cars and the Golden Gate Bridge. Cleveland is a gray place with a lot of industrial smokestacks.

Obviously, London, Paris, and Rome are all top-of-the-ladder destinations that are most popular with first-time travelers to Europe. Sabena had little chance to get these travelers.

But in the United States there is a large segment of seasoned travelers looking to visit the next tier of destinations. Countries like Greece with its ruins. Switzerland with its mountains.

Once the objective became clear, finding a position wasn't that difficult.

Beautiful Belgium

Belgium is a beautiful country with many of the things that appeal to the seasoned European traveler. Like interesting cities, historical palaces, museums, and art galleries.

Oddly enough, many Belgian people don't have a high opinion of their own country as a tourist attraction. That attitude is perhaps epitomized by a sign that used to be at the Brussels airport. Among other things it said, "Welcome to Belga country. Weather: mild, but rains 220 days a year, on average."

As the result, Belgium's favorite tourist strategy was to promote the central location of Brussels as a "gateway" city and the ease of getting somewhere else. Like London, Paris, and Rome. (If you want to visit New York, fly to Philadelphia because it's close by.)

There's an important lesson here. The perceptions of people living in a place are often different from those visiting it.

Many New Yorkers fail to see New York as a tourist attraction. They remember the garbage strikes and forget the Statue of Liberty. Yet New York attracts 16 million visitors a year who all want to see those "big buildings."

Three-star cities

But while "beautiful" was a good position, it wasn't really enough as a tourist promotion theme. To position a country as a destination, you need attractions that will keep the traveler around for at least a few days.

Nobody considers Monaco much of a destination because its number one attraction, Monte Carlo, can be seen in an evening.

Obviously, size is an important factor. Big countries have lots of attractions. Small countries are at a disadvantage. (If the Grand Canyon ran through Belgium, you wouldn't have much land left to look at.)

We found the answer to the overall positioning problem in one of those Michelin Guides. You may not know that Michelin rates cities as well as restaurants.

Michelin's Benelux edition lists six three-star "worth a special journey" cities. Five were in Belgium: Bruges, Ghent, Antwerp, Brussels, and Tournai.

But what was really surprising was the fact that the big tourist attraction to the North, Holland, had only one three-star city, Amsterdam.

The ad that resulted was headlined, "In beautiful Belgium, there are five Amsterdams." The illustration was comprised of five beautiful four-color pictures of Belgium's three-star cities.

This advertisement generated an enormous number of inquiries about a country many travelers had seen only through the train window as they traveled from Amsterdam to Paris.

One of the inquiries came in the form of a call from the minister of tourism in Holland to his counterpart in Belgium. Needless to say, there was one irate Dutchman who wanted that advertisement killed, along with the people who created it.

The "three-star city" strategy had three important things going for it.

First, it related Belgium to a destination that was already in the mind of the traveler, Amsterdam. In any positioning program, if you can start with a strongly held perception, you'll be that much ahead in your efforts to establish your own position.

Second, the Michelin Guide, another entity already in the mind of the traveler, gave the concept credibility.

Finally, the "five cities to visit" made Belgium a bona fide destination.

Eventually the "three-star cities of beautiful Belgium" concept was moved into television. The response was substantial.

A television commercial with its ability to communicate in sight and sound can drive pictures of a country into the mind much more quickly than a print advertisement.

There's also a danger of misusing the medium of television. This happens when your visuals are similar to visuals being used by other countries.

Think about those islands in the Caribbean you've seen advertised. Can you keep those palm trees and beaches separate in your mind? Do you conjure up the same mental postcard when someone says Nassau, the Virgin Islands, or Barbados? If there's no difference, the mind will simply dump all those visuals in a slot marked "Islands in the Caribbean" and tune out.

The same thing can happen with those quaint European villages. Or the smiling residents waving mugs of beer at you. We solved the problem by using the Michelin "stars" as if they were church bells which rang out as they were superimposed on the Belgium city scenes.

What happened?

Now you might be wondering why, after all this, you haven't seen much about Belgium and its three-star cities.

A number of events kept this program from getting off the ground. All of which holds a lesson for anyone embarked on a positioning program.

New management not committed to the program arrived on the scene, and when headquarters in Brussels wanted to change the strategy, they quickly acquiesced.

The lesson here is that a successful positioning program requires a major long-term commitment by the people in charge. Whether it's the head of a corporation, a church, an airline, or a country.

In a constantly changing political environment, this is difficult to accomplish.

16 Positioning an island: Jamaica

When Edward Seaga replaced socialist Michael Manley as Jamaican prime minister, he proclaimed an open door for capitalist investment.

David Rockefeller was so impressed, he formed a group of 25 American corporate chiefs specifically for the purpose of developing Jamaica. In the due course of events the Jamaicans, encouraged by the Rockefeller committee, hired us to develop a position for the island of Jamaica.

Investment or tourism?

Jamaica at the time needed both. But which should come first?

Obviously, investments won't do much for tourism, but many tourists work for big companies. If they come back from Jamaica with favorable impressions, they just might encourage their companies to invest in the island. Executives at those same companies like to invest in places that are fun to visit. Which is why you see so little investment in Alaska and so much in the Caribbean.

Who wants to go to Fairbanks in the wintertime to check out the plant?

The competition

Looking at the Caribbean from a tourist's point of view, there are four major competitors to Jamaica: the Bahamas, Puerto Rico, the U.S. Virgin Islands, and Bermuda. Each of these destinations draws more visitors a year than Jamaica.

What springs to mind when you mention any of these Caribbean islands? With one exception, the consistent visual image is the couple in the bathing suits on the beach, underneath the palm trees. (This sea, sand, and surf picture has become a visual cliché for the Caribbean.)

The exception, of course, is Bermuda. Years of advertising those motorbikes parked beside the pink sand have put a strong visual in the mind.

Effective, too. Our research shows that in terms of perceptions, Bermuda is second in desirability to the U.S. Virgin Islands. If it weren't for the weather factor (Bermuda is considerably north of the other islands), Bermuda would have been in first place.

Jamaica's positioning problem is similar to the problem of Belgium. How to put a mental picture postcard into the mind of the Caribbean prospect?

The search for the postcard

The first approach is to sort through thousands of postcards to find the one perfect picture of the island of Jamaica. But it can't be found.

There's a good reason. If there were one image that captured the essense of the island, someone would have noticed it already and used it. In other words, there would have been an image already burned into at least a few minds.

The second approach is to visit Jamaica and shoot hundreds or thousands of pictures trying to capture that illusive mental picture postcard. Not surprisingly, nothing totally right turns up.

The third approach is the one that should have been used first. It's to look into the mind of the prospect to see what mental images already exist. And then select one you can tie Jamaica into.

What is the verbal essence of Jamaica? An old advertisement said, "Jamaica is the big green island in the Caribbean that has deserted beaches, cool mountains, country pastures, open plains, rivers, rapids, waterfalls, ponds, good drinking water, and a jungly interior."

Does that sound familiar? Does it remind you of a very popular tourist destination in the Pacific?

The Hawaiian connection

That's right. Hawaii. Most people have a mental picture of the big green volcanic mountains coming down to the blue sea.

It's a view that you can also see as you approach the island of Jamaica, the Hawaii of the Caribbean.

The Hawaii of the Caribbean becomes an even more powerful concept when you compare Jamaica with its four biggest competitors. This chart lists the highest point of each destination.

Bermuda	259 feet
Bahamas	400 feet
U.S. Virgin Islands	1556 feet
Puerto Rico	4389 feet
Jamaica	7402 feet

At 7402 feet, Blue Mountain in Jamaica is higher than any point in the United States east of the Mississippi River.

Another important comparison is the size of each destination. This chart gives the length of the largest island in each destination.

Bermuda	4 miles
Bahamas	8 miles
U.S. Virgin Islands	7½ miles
Puerto Rico	50 miles
Jamaica	62½ miles

Again, Jamaica is considerably larger than any of its competitors. Jamaica has hundreds of miles of beaches and two volcanic mountain ranges with a towering peak over 7000 feet. This supports the "More to see, more to do" advantages that are also implicit in the Hawaiian connection.

Conceptually, this approach says to tourists that the things they travel a great distance to Hawaii for (natural beauty, big green mountains, beautiful beaches, wonderful year-round weather) can be found a lot closer to home, down in the Caribbean.

Jamaica could even copy one of the most successful of Hawaii's marketing ploys: meeting tourists with flowers at the airport.

Jamaica has beautiful flowers and this gesture, above all, would say that Jamaica is a friendly place as well as a beautiful one.

Benefits of the "Hawaiian" position

"The Hawaii of the Caribbean" provides a quick visual analogy. Jamaica doesn't have the luxury of building that visual image over the years. Transferring Hawaii's mental picture postcards will save enormous amounts of time and money.

Furthermore, the concept strongly differentiates Jamaica from the other Caribbean destinations.

A poster entitled "A cartographer's view of the Caribbean" made this point very graphically. It showed each of the destinations drawn to scale. (You need a magnifying glass to find Bermuda.)

Another major benefit of the Hawaiian analogy is the platform it provides for European programs. If you live on the Continent, Hawaii is a long way away.

If you're wondering why you haven't heard much about the Hawaii of the Caribbean, you'll have to ask Mr. Seaga. He is widely viewed as a Caribbean Ronald Reagan, but "he is really the Jimmy Carter of Jamaica," a Rockefeller aide told *The Wall Street Journal*. "He's the person who gets involved in every detail and agonizes over every issue."

Presumably he is still agonizing over this one.

17 Positioning a product: Milk Duds

The brand is Milk Duds, a product of Switzer Clark. Milk Duds is a candy product that comes in a little yellow and brown box. It had a reputation as a "movie" candy for teenagers, but the company wanted to broaden its Milk Duds business to include the younger crowd.

Looking into the mind

The first step in any positioning program is to look inside the mind of the prospect.

And who is the prospect for Milk Duds? It's not some little kid who doesn't know the score. Research indicates that the best Milk Duds prospect is a sophisticated candy buyer. He or she has been in and out of candy stores several hundred times at least.

The average Milk Duds prospect is 10 years old. A cautious, suspicious, shrewd purchasing agent who is always on the look-out for value received.

Most positioning programs are nothing more or less than a search for the obvious. Yet the obvious is easy to miss if you zero in too quickly on the product itself. (As with the "pur-loined letter" of Edgar Allan Poe, the obvious is often hard to find because it's too easy to see. It's too obvious.)

What's in the prospect's mind when the subject of candy comes up? Not Milk Duds, even though the average 10-year-old kid might be vaguely aware of the brand.

For most 10-year-olds, the candy urge immediately conjures up the concept of candy bars.

Candy bars like Hersheys, Nestlés, Mounds, Almond Joys, Reeses, Snickers, Milky Ways. Put there, of course, by the millions of dollars' worth of advertising spent on these and other candy bar brands.

Repositioning the competition

Since Milk Duds was getting only a small fraction of that kind of advertising money, it would have been hopeless to try to build a separate identity for the brand. The only way to drive Milk Duds into the kid's mind was to find a way to reposition the candy bar category.

In other words, find a way to make the millions of dollars spent by the competition work for Milk Duds by setting up the brand as an alternative to the candy bar. (Little would be gained by just putting another candy name in an overloaded mind.)

Fortunately, there was a glaring weakness in the candy bar competition that could be exploited. And the weakness is obvious once you look at the size and shape and price of today's Hershey bar.

A candy bar just doesn't last very long. A kid can go through a 50-cent Hershey bar in 2.3 seconds flat.

There exists a strong undercurrent of dissatisfaction among America's candy eaters. As the candy bar has shrunk in size, this discontent has grown.

"My allowance doesn't last very long when it comes to candy bars."

"Either I'm eating faster or candy bars are getting smaller."

"You can suck up a candy bar awfully fast these days!"

This is the soft, chocolaty underbelly of the candy bar competition.

Milk Duds are different. They come in a box instead of a package. They give the kid 15 individual slow-eating chocolate-covered caramels.

Compared with a candy bar, a box of Milk Duds will last a long time. (If you try to stuff a whole box in your mouth, it will cement your jaws shut.) Which is exactly why the product has been so popular in movie theaters.

So what is Milk Duds' new position?

The long-lasting alternative

Why, it's America's long-lasting alternative to the candy bar.

If this seems like the obvious answer to you, it wasn't to the people who used to do the Milk Duds advertising. In some 15 years of Milk Duds' television commercials, there wasn't one reference to the long-lasting idea.

Let's take a mental walk through a 30-second television commercial to see how the long-lasting idea was sugarcoated for the benefit of the 10-year-old.

1. Once there was a kid who had a big mouth . . . (A kid is standing next to an enormous mouth.)
2. . . . that loved candy bars. (The kid is shoveling candy bars one right after another into the mouth.)
3. . . . but they didn't last very long. (The kid runs out of candy bars and the mouth gets very upset.)
4. Then he discovered chocolaty caramel Milk Duds. (The kid holds up the Milk Duds, and the mouth starts to lick its chops.)
5. The mouth loved the Milk Duds because they last a long time. (The kid rolls the Milk Duds one by one up the mouth's tongue.)
6. (Then the kid and the mouth sing a duet together, which is the campaign song.) When a candy bar is only a memory, you'll still be eating your Milk Duds.
7. Get your mouth some Milk Duds. (Big smiles on both the kid and the mouth.)

Did it work?

Not only did the television advertising reverse a downward sales trend, but in the ensuing months the company sold more Milk Duds than it ever did in its history.

If there is one important lesson to be learned from the Milk Duds example, it's this: The solution to a positioning problem is usually found in the prospect's mind, not in the product.

18 Positioning a service: Mailgram

What's the difference between the positioning of a product (like Milk Duds) and the positioning of a service (like Western Union's Mailgram)?

Not much, especially from a strategic point of view. Most of the differences are in techniques.

Visual vs. verbal

In a product ad, the dominant element is usually the picture, the visual element. In a service ad, the dominant element is usually the words, the verbal element. (So if you saw an advertisement with a big picture of an automobile, you would assume the car was being advertised, not a car rental service.)

With a product like Milk Duds, the primary medium was television, a visually oriented vehicle.

With a service like Mailgram, the primary medium was radio, a verbally oriented vehicle.

Naturally, there are a lot of exceptions to these principles. If everyone knows what the product looks like, there is no advantage in using print, television, or other forms of visual media.

Conversely, if a service can make effective use of a visual symbol (O. J. Simpson for Hertz, for example), then visual media can often be productive.

In spite of the exceptions, it's surprising how often these visual/verbal generalities hold up. In a four-way test of newspapers, magazines, radio, and television for Mailgram, the most effective medium was radio. But the essence of the Mailgram story is strategy, not media. Before discussing strategy, it may be helpful to take a look at how the system works.

Electronic mail

Developed jointly with the U.S. Postal Service and inaugurated on a limited experimental basis in 1970, Mailgram is the nation's first electronic mail.

To send a Mailgram, you call Western Union, which transmits the message electronically to a post office near the recipient. The Mailgram is delivered the next business day.

In addition to sending Mailgrams by telephone, the customer can also send them by telex, TWX, magnetic tape, computer, facsimile equipment, or communicating typewriters.

Why belabor the technicalities? Why discuss the complex details of the Mailgram system?

To make an important point. Most advertising programs never go beyond the details of the product or service which is offered for sale. And the more interesting and complex the service is, the more likely this will happen. The marketing people who are responsible for introducing the product get all wrapped up in the service and forget all about the customer. As a matter of fact, the traditional approach would have been to introduce Mailgram as a "new, automated, computerized electronic communication service" or something of that sort. (Western Union spent millions on computer programming alone, not to mention the enormous expense of earth stations, satellites, etc.)

The low-cost telegram

Regardless of how much money you spend, regardless of how technologically interesting your service is, to get inside the prospect's mind, you have to relate to what's already there. You can't walk away from your existing position in the prospect's mind.

And what's up there in the prospect's mind? The Telegram, of course.

Anytime you mention the word "Western Union," the average mind conjures up the most famous yellow message in the history of the world. And the "gram" part of the Mailgram name only reinforces this perception.

So what's the difference between the new gram and the old gram?

Well, the main difference is price. Both have the same telegraphic format. Both demand immediate attention. But the yellow Telegram message is three times the price of the blue and white Mailgram message.

So the positioning theme developed for Mailgram was simple: "Mailgram: Impact of a Telegram at a fraction of the cost."

At this point, someone said "Wait a minute. Why position Mailgram against the Telegram, also a Western Union service? Why take business away from ourselves?

"Furthermore, the Telegram is a declining business. Why compare a new, modern service like Mailgram with an old service past its prime? The Telegram still has an important role to play, but it is not a growth business."

The logic is impeccable. But as often happens, logic is not necessarily the best strategy for dealing with human minds. Still, the logic was so sound, it was worthwhile rethinking the concept. Especially since there was another positioning strategy that also had merit.

The high-speed letter

Actually the Mailgram name itself suggests a second positioning approach. We could relate the Mailgram to the U.S. mail.

Then, too, if Western Union wanted the Mailgram to take business away from another service, the numbers suggest it would be much better to position the service against regular mail.

In a recent year, 68 billion first-class letters were dropped into the nation's letter boxes. That's 815 first-class letters per household per year.

The Telegram generates only a tiny fraction of that kind of volume.

So a second theme was developed: "Mailgram: A new high-speed service for important messages."

Which is the better approach? In spite of the negatives, positioning theory suggests that the "low-cost Telegram" is a better direction than the "high-speed letter." Yet Mailgram was too important to Western Union to make a decision based on judgment alone. So both campaigns were test-marketed using computer data to track results.

Low cost vs. high speed

The test itself was a massive one. No tiny markets like Peoria were even considered. The six Mailgram test cities were Boston, Chicago, Houston, Los Angeles, Philadelphia, and San Francisco. All big, important communication centers.

Who won? Actually both campaigns were effective. Here are the data for Mailgram volume increases in the test cities during the 13-week program.

High-speed letter cities	plus 73%
Low-cost Telegram cities	plus 100%

These numbers alone were enough to prove the superiority of the "low-cost Telegram" position. But what really decided the issue were the product awareness levels in the test cities, which were measured both before the program ran and afterward.

Here are the figures on how many people could correctly describe what a Mailgram was before the print and broadcast advertising began

High-speed letter cities	27%
Low-cost Telegram cities	23%

Statistically, not much difference. This indicates that the test market cities were pretty evenly matched. In other words, about one-fourth of the market already knew about the Mailgram service.

After the advertising ran, however, there was a big difference in the two groups of cities. Here are the Mailgram awareness levels 13 weeks later.

High-speed letter cities	25%
Low-cost Telegram cities	47%

As unbelievable as it may seem, awareness in the high-speed letter cities actually declined. From 27 percent to 25 percent. (Not really statistically significant.)

Then where did the increased volume come from in the high-speed letter cities? Obviously from people who knew what a Mailgram was and were reminded to use the service by the advertising.

It was a totally different story in the low-cost Telegram cities. Mailgram awareness more than doubled. From 23 percent to 47 percent.

Not only was this a big jump, but the numbers suggest that Mailgram volume increases were likely to continue over a long period of time.

Western Union also measured Telegram volume in the test cities before, during, and after the advertising. They found that volume held fairly stable. In fact, the company felt that advertising the Mailgram as the low-cost Telegram helped rather than hurt Telegram volume.

And what has happened to Mailgram since the development of this advertising strategy? The volume numbers tell the story.

1972 . . . . .6 million	1977 . . . . .28 million
1973 . . . . .11 million	1978 . . . . .33 million
1974 . . . . .20 million	1979 . . . . .37 million
1975 . . . . .23 million	1980 . . . . .39 million
1976 . . . . .25 million	1981 . . . . .41 million

After 10 years of success, Western Union decided to change the Mailgram strategy. Instead of "impact," the new strategy would emphasize "next-day delivery." So they hired a new advertising agency to develop the new program.

Again, the volume numbers tell the story.

| 1981 . . . . .41 million |
| 1982 . . . . .37 million |
| 1983 . . . . .30 million |
| 1984 . . . . .22 million |

Rarely can you find such a clearcut example of the difference between good advertising strategy and bad. (Most examples are clouded by other factors.) But in the Mailgram case, the minute the strategy was changed, volume declined.

Your problem is not just one of developing a good strategy. Equally important is the courage you will need to keep hammering at the same theme, year after year.

19

Positioning a Long Island bank

Like Western Union, banks sell a service and not a product. Unlike a Mailgram, however, which is a national service, banking is still a regional service.

In fact, positioning a bank is much like positioning a department store, an appliance store, or any other kind of retail establishment. To successfully position a retail outlet, you must know the territory.

The Long Island banking situation

To understand how we developed a position for the Long Island Trust Company, you should know a little bit about the territory.

For many years Long Island Trust was the leading bank on the Island. It was the largest bank, it had the most branches, and it made the most money.

In the seventies, however, the bank battlefield on Long Island changed dramatically. A new law permitted unrestricted branch banking throughout New York State.

Since then, many of the big New York City banks have become firmly entrenched in the Long Island area. Banks like Citibank, Chase Manhattan, and Chemical Bank.

Also, a good number of Long Island's residents commute to New York City everyday and do part of their banking at these same banks.

However, the intrusion of the big city banks into Long Island Trust's territory was only part of the problem. The territory that really counts is in the mind of the banking prospect. And a little research turned up a lot of bad news.

Mapping the prospect's mind

By now you can appreciate the importance of knowing what's in the prospect's mind. Not only about your product or service, but about competitive offerings as well.

Often the insights are intuitive. Nobody needs a $20,000 research project to know that Western Union is strongly identified with the Telegram. Nor was much research needed to determine the positions of Milk Duds, Belgium, and Xerox.

More often than not, however, it can be exceedingly helpful to map the prospect's mind by means of formal positioning research. Helpful not only in developing a strategy, but in selling the strategy to top management. (The chief executive who has spent 30 years with one company will obviously see that company differently than a prospect whose total exposure over the same 30 years can be measured in minutes or even seconds.)

"Mapping the prospect's mind" is normally done with a research technique called "semantic differential." This was the procedure used to develop a positioning program for the Long Island Trust Company.

In semantic differential research, the prospect is given a set of attributes and then asked to rank each competitor on a scale, generally from 1 to 10.

For example, price might be one of the attributes. In automobiles, it's obvious that Cadillac would be ranked at the high end and Chevette at the low end.

In banking, there is almost no price perception, so other attributes were selected. The ones chosen were these: (1) many branches, (2) full range of services, (3) quality of service, (4) large capital, (5) helps Long Island residents, and (6) helps Long Island economy.

The first four attributes are the traditional reasons for doing business with a particular bank. The last two are unique to the Long Island situation.

As far as the traditional reasons were concerned, the situation was bleak for the Long Island Trust. Prospects rated them last on all four attributes.

Many branches

Chemical 7.3
National Bank of North America 6.7
European American 6.6
Chase Manhattan 6.4
Citibank 6.1
Long Island Trust 5.4

Full range of services

Chemical 7.7
Citibank 7.7
Chase Manhattan 7.6
National Bank of North America 7.4
European American 7.3
Long Island Trust 7.0

Quality of service

Chemical 7.2
Citibank 7.0
National Bank of North America 7.0
Chase Manhattan 6.9
European American 6.8
Long Island Trust 6.7

Large capital

Chemical	8.2
Chase Manhattan	8.2
Citibank	8.1
National Bank of North America	7.8
European American	7.7
Long Island Trust	7.1

The positions were reversed, however, when the attributes concerned Long Island itself.

Here is how the respondents ranked the six banks on the Long Island attributes.

Helps Long Island residents

Long Island Trust	7.5
National Bank of North America	6.6
European American	5.2
Chemical	5.1
Chase Manhattan	4.7
Citibank	4.5

Helps Long Island economy

Long Island Trust	7.3
National Bank of North America	6.7
European American	5.4
Chemical	5.4
Citibank	5.3
Chase Manhattan	4.9

When the attributes concerned Long Island, the Long Island Trust Company went right to the top. A not too surprising result, considering the power of the name.

Developing the strategy

What approach should Long Island Trust take? Conventional wisdom says you accept your strengths and work on improving your weaknesses. In other words, run ads telling the prospects about the great service, friendly tellers, etc.

Conventional wisdom is not positioning thinking. Positioning theory says you must start with what the prospect is already willing to give you.

And the only thing the prospect gave Long Island Trust was the "Long Island position." Accepting this position allowed the bank to repel the invasion of the big city banks. The first ad stated the theme.

Why send your money to the city if you live on the Island?

It makes sense to keep your money close to home. Not at a city bank. But at Long Island Trust. Where it can work for Long Island.

After all, we concentrate on developing Long Island.

Not Manhattan Island. Or some island off Kuwait.

Ask yourself, who do you think is most concerned about Long Island's future?

A bank-come-lately with hundreds of other branches in the greater metropolitan area plus affiliates in five continents?

Or a bank like ours that's been here for over 50 years and has 33 offices on Long Island.

A second ad had a photo of palm trees in front of a building with a Citibank N.A. sign.

To a big city bank, a branch in Nassau isn't necessarily your Nassau.

Chances are it will turn out to be in the Bahamas. It's one of the favorite locations of the big city banks. In fact, the multinational institutions have some $75 billion in loans booked in the Bahamas and Cayman Islands.

Nothing wrong with that. Except it doesn't do much for you if Long Island is your home.

Long Island is not only our favorite location, it's our only location. We have 18 branches in Nassau (County, that is) and 16 in Queens and Suffolk.

And we've been here a long time, over a half century. We're involved financially to the extent that 95 percent of our loans and services go to Long Islanders and their homes, schools, and businesses.

Other ads in the campaign had similar themes:

"The city is a great place to visit, but would you want to bank there?"

"To a city bank, the only island that really counts is Manhattan." (A tiny drawing of Long Island is dwarfed by an enormous drawing of Manhattan.)

"If times get tough, will the city banks get going? (Back to the city.)"

Fifteen months later the same research was repeated. Notice how Long Island Trust's position improved in every attribute.

Many branches

Long Island Trust	7.0
National Bank of North America	6.8
Chemical	6.6
Citibank	6.5
Chase Manhattan	6.1
European American	6.1

From last to first place in "many branches." In spite of the fact that Chemical Bank, for example, has more than twice as many branches on Long Island.

Full range of services

Citibank	7.8
Chemical	7.8
Chase Manhattan	7.6
Long Island Trust	7.3
National Bank of North America	7.3
European American	7.2

In "full range of services" Long Island Trust moved up two spots. From sixth to fourth place.

Quality of service

Citibank	7.8
Chemical	7.6
Chase Manhattan	7.5
Long Island Trust	7.1
National Bank of North America	7.1
European American	7.0

In "quality of service" Long Island Trust also moved from sixth to fourth place.

Large capital

Long Island Trust	7.0
Chemical	6.7
Citibank	6.7
National Bank of North America	6.6
Chase Manhattan	6.6
European American	6.4

In "large capital" Long Island Trust moved from last to first place.

Results were seen not only in the research but in the branches too. "With the assistance of the advertising agency which pioneered the widely accepted concept of positioning," said the bank's annual report, "our lead bank, Long Island Trust, assumed the mantle of the Long Island Bank for Long Islanders. Acceptance of the campaign was immediate and gratifying."

You might think that a bank promoting the area that it serves is an obvious idea. And it is.

But the best positioning ideas are so simple and obvious that most people overlook them.

20 Positioning a New Jersey bank

The bank is United Jersey with 116 branches in the state of New Jersey.

United Jersey is not in the same situation as Long Island Trust. (There is no one positioning approach that will work everywhere.) There are many differences between the two banks, the most important being that unlike Long Island Trust, United Jersey is not the biggest local bank in its marketing territory. (That distinction belongs to First Fidelity with Midlantic in second place and United Jersey in third.)

Finding a viable banking position

One thing that United Jersey has in common with Long Island Trust is its marketing environment. Both operate in the shadows of Citibank, Chase Manhattan, Chemical, Manufacturers Hanover, and the other big New York City banks. That's at the north end of the territory.

In the south, United Jersey operates in the shadows of the big Philadelphia banks (Mellon, First Pennsylvania).

The problem of finding a viable banking position is complicated by the fact that the services offered by United Jersey are similar to those of its competitors. Federal and state regulations see to that.

The only approach that will work is the Tylenol approach. You don't find the answer to the problem of positioning the bank by studying the bank. You find it by studying the competition, as Tylenol did by studying the problems of aspirin.

At one end of the scale, United Jersey competes in the marketing jungle known as metropolitan New York City.

And it really is a banking jungle. In Manhattan alone, there are 389 banks. Not to mention Brooklyn, Queens, the Bronx, Staten Island, and the entire state of New Jersey.

The King and Queen of the jungle are Citibank and Chase Manhattan. These are big banks. In Manhattan alone Citibank has 74 branches.

How do you find weakness in Citibank, which has almost as many vice presidents as United Jersey has employees?

The disadvantage of large size

The problem of finding a meaningful advantage for United Jersey can be approached by looking at the disadvantages of its big-city competitors.

Why position United Jersey against the big banks? Why not take on the score of small financial institutions? The reason to go against the big banks is because they are the ones in the minds of the prospects. Positioning is always a question of dealing with what's in the mind.

The disadvantage of large size is slow service. As an Avis ad once said, "Rent from us. The line at our counter is shorter." Banks shouldn't hold up people, either. We developed a positioning strategy for United Jersey called the "fast-moving bank." This strategy had two key aspects.

A. Exploit the only real weakness of the big metropolitan New York banks: their slow reaction time.

B. Encourage United Jersey management to make sure the bank's performance matches the advertising's promise. That took the form of seven key commitments.

1. **Decentralized decisions.** United Jersey pushed decision making down to the local level. (One of their lending teams can approve a $10 million loan, and that team meets daily.) In 10 commercial banking centers throughout the state, other officers on site can make business loans quickly.

2. **Cross training.** United Jersey trains its people in all their banking services, not just in one specialty. So when a customer has a question, he or she doesn't have to wait for an answer while the question is referred to another person.

3. **Commitment to electronics.** United Jersey's system of statewide ATMs (Automatic Teller Machines) is the largest private network in the state. United Jersey's corporate customers can be on line directly with the bank's computers for balance inquiries and other daily questions.

4. **Speedy lock box service.** United Jersey people pick up checks six times a day during the workweek, four times on the weekend. Its Newark lock box has its own private ZIP Code. United Jersey empties lock boxes and fills up customer accounts as fast as it can.

5. **FACT terminals.** (Fast Authorization of Cashless Transactions.) With these terminals now in place, merchants enjoy the benefit of rapid electronic approvals. And faster approvals with minimized risk mean improved cash flow.

6. **Responsiveness.** Whether it's being first with a new product or matching the competition's rates, United Jersey is committed to being responsive to the customer's financial needs.

7. **Central location.** United Jersey built its new corporate headquarters in Princeton. From the geographic center of the state, United Jersey is less than an hour away from any of its business customers by car, even less by helicopter.

Advertising the fast-moving bank

When the bank's performance matched the promises the advertising was going to make, the advertising started to make the
promises. Focusing on the weakness of the competition,
naturally.

Each television spot contrasted United Jersey bankers with
their counterparts at the whimsically named "Lethargic
National Bank." In one spot, approval for a business loan at
Lethargic National seemed to take forever. A second spot
showed a Lethargic banker disappearing when a customer
needed a quick answer to his questions. And in the third spot,
a husband and wife found the bankers at Lethargic moving in
slow motion on a simple installment loan.

The humorous vignettes drove home the point that United
Jersey "values your time as much as your money."

Print advertisements also carried the "fast-moving bank"
theme. "Haste makes money" and "Banks shouldn't hold up
people," were two typical headlines.

"Time Is Money" desk signs were given to all United Jersey
bank officers, a not-so-subtle reminder not to keep the customer sitting next to their desk waiting.

Did it work?

By all measurements the fast-moving bank strategy was a big
success for United Jersey. Unaided awareness, for example,
almost tripled in just over a year.

Business and profits went up. A year after the program
started, United Jersey announced earnings were up $30 mil-
lion, an increase of 26 percent over the previous year.

An even more important barometer of change was the attitude of employees. One United Jersey officer reported, "The
image advertising is great, but the best thing I've seen happen
is that our people, line officers, etc., are striving to live up to
Fast Moving . . . and they are! I've seen a tremendous change

in attitude since the campaign began. Approvals come faster. People don't sit on things."

The essence of a good positioning strategy is that it transcends every aspect of a company. You know you have a winner when you run it up the corporate flagpole and everybody salutes.

21
Positioning a ski resort: Stowe

There are over a thousand "name" ski areas in America. Since the mind of the average skier can hold only a fraction of those names, the problem of positioning a ski resort can be difficult.

If your name is Stowe, the problem is greatly simplified. Stowe is already well known. "Stowe is for me the essential Eastern ski village," said *Advertising Age* columnist James Brady, "the way Aspen is out west or Val d'Isere is in France or Kitzbühel is in Austria."

Why a position for Stowe?

With that kind of reputation, why does Stowe need a position? Isn't it enough to advertise Stowe and let the skier conjure up the Stowe image?

To a certain extent, this is true. The reputation of a product like Steinway or a place like Stowe creates word of mouth which carries the reputation along from year to year. But proper positioning can enhance the word of mouth and contribute to the process. In essence, the positioning supplies the material to talk about.

What do skiers talk about? James Brady put it best. They talk about places to ski, places like Aspen, Val d'Isere, and Kitzbühel.

With this background in mind, the search began for a position for Stowe. The situation seemed to call for the outside expert, the person who could supply the credibility to bring a comparison claim to life.

The top 10 ski resorts in the world

The noted ski and travel writer, Abby Rand, supplied the credibility. Writing in *Harper's Bazaar*, she selected the top 10 ski resorts in the world. One was Stowe, Vermont. The others were: Aspen, Colorado; Courchevel, France; Jackson Hole, Wyoming; Kitzbühel, Austria; Portillo, Chile; St. Christoph, Austria; St. Moritz, Switzerland; Sun Valley, Idaho; and Vail, Colorado. (Not a bad list.)

The positioning advertisements for Stowe used shoulder patches to illustrate the ski areas. "Of the world's top 10 ski resorts," said the ad, "only one is in the East."

"You don't have to go to the Alps or the Andes or even to the Rockies to experience the ski vacation of a lifetime," continued the ad. "You need only head for the Ski Capital of the East: Stowe, Vermont."

Skiers responded to the new Stowe strategy. They requested thousands of brochures in response to the advertising. They also broke all attendance records at the ski resort.

You might think it would be easy to increase business at a place like Stowe, but competition has one major advantage. Places like Stratton, Sugarbush, Big Bromley, and Mt. Snow are all located south of Stowe. So the skier driving from the major population center (New York City) has to drive an hour or two longer to get to Stowe. One of the functions of the advertising is to promise the skier a reward for the longer drive.

"One of the top 10 ski resorts in the world" is a classic positioning strategy. It takes advantage of the mind's tendency to "make a list" when trying to cope with complexity. "The seven wonders of the world" is one of the earliest examples of this approach.

Furthermore, the "top 10" strategy can conceivably be used indefinitely. There's no reason to change. What better strategy can there be than having your place or product included in a list of the world's best?

When you use a recognized authority to give your product or service credibility, you are tapping a fundamental aspect of human nature. There's security in not having to trust your own judgment.

The dark side of this tendency to defer to authority was explored by Allen Funt, creator of *Candid Camera*. "The worst thing, and I see it over and over," said Mr. Funt, "is how easily people can be led by one kind of authority or even the most minimal signs of authority."

"We put up a sign on the road, *Delaware Closed Today*," reported Mr. Funt. "Motorists didn't question it. Instead they asked, 'Is Jersey open?'"

22 Positioning the Catholic Church

This book could have been written about religion just as well as about advertising.

A farfetched idea?

Not really. The essence of any religion is communication. From divinity to clergy to congregation.

The problems arise not with a perfect divinity or an imperfect congregation but with the clergy.

How the clergy applies communication theory to the practice of religion will have a major influence on the way religion affects the congregation.

An identity crisis

Some years ago, positioning thinking was applied to the Catholic Church. In other words, communication problems of this enormous institution were treated as if they belonged to a major corporation.

This request did not come from the Pope or a committee of bishops. It came from a group of laity who were deeply concerned about what one renowned theologian dubbed a "certain crisis of identity" that had followed in the wake of the reforms of Vatican II.

It was quickly apparent that communication in the Catholic Church was haphazard at best.

While much effort had been expended in improving techniques, the programs lacked a strong central theme or any continuity. (An especially serious problem in an era of electronic overcommunication.)

It was like General Motors with no overall corporate advertising programs. All communication came from the local dealers. Some of it good, much of it bad.

A large measure of the problems could be traced to Vatican II.

Prior to that "opening of the windows," the institutional Church had a clearly perceived position in the minds of the faithful. To most, the Church was the teacher of the law. Much emphasis was placed on rules, rewards, and punishment. The Church was consistent in its approach to old and young alike.

Vatican II moved the Catholic Church away from this posture of law and order. Many rules and regulations were dismissed as unnecessary. Changes in liturgy and style became commonplace. Flexibility took the place of rigidity.

Unfortunately, there was no advertising manager in Rome when these momentous changes were being made. No one to distill what had transpired and produce a program in simple language that explained the new directions.

After years of not needing a "corporate" communication program, it's understandable that the Catholic Church failed to recognize the scope of the problem on its hands.

Losing its influence

What was painfully lacking was a clear presentation of what the new church was about.

The faithful quietly asked, "If you are not the teacher of the law, what are you?"

In the years since Vatican II, there has been no simple answer forthcoming. No attempt to reposition the church in the minds of the laity. Even in the minds of the clergy, for that matter.

And with no answers, confusion walked in and many people walked out.

For the first time, regular Mass attendance dropped below 50 percent of the Catholic population. This amounts to a 20 percent drop, while Protestant attendance has remained remarkably stable.

There are 20 percent fewer priests, nuns, and brothers today than there were 10 years ago. Vocations have dropped by 60 percent.

One final set of statistics is especially significant. The Catholic Church is presently the "largest community of moral authority in American society." (A title bestowed upon it by the Protestant theologian Peter Berger.)

Yet when a group of 24,000 highly influential executives were asked by *U.S. News & World Report* to rate the influence of major institutions, the Church and other organized religions came in dead last.

The moral authority of the Catholic Church was obviously not being communicated very well.

What role for the Church?

"What is the role of the Catholic Church in the modern world?"

This question was asked of clergy, bishops, laity. Never was the same answer received twice.

Some say there is no simple answer. Some say there's more than one answer. (Recognize the everybody trap.)

Corporate executives usually have answers to questions like this. If you ask the top executives at General Motors, they will more than likely see their role as being the world's largest manufacturer of automobiles. Companies spend millions finding and communicating the essence of their products with words like "Whiter than white" or "Fighting cavities is what Crest is all about."

The Church had to answer this unanswered question in simple, definitive terms. And it had to put this answer into a totally integrated communication program. Then it had to take this program to the flock in a new and dramatic way.

Working out an identity program for a corporation usually entails a retracing of steps until you discover the basic business of a company. This requires poring over old plans and programs. Seeing what worked and what didn't.

In the case of the Catholic Church, you have to go back 2000 years and retrace the steps of the Church. Instead of old annual reports, you have to rely on Scripture.

In the search for a simple, direct expression of the role of the Church, two explicit statements in the Gospel could hold the answer.

First, during Christ's ministry on earth, God, as reported in Matthew's Gospel, instructed man to listen to the words of his Son, the Beloved (Matt. 17:23).

Then Christ, as he departed from earth, instructed his followers to go and teach all nations what they had heard from him (Matt. 28:19).

Teacher of the word

It's apparent from the Scriptures that Christ saw the role of the Church as "teacher of the word."

Because he was "the Son of God," it must be assumed that his word is a word for all ages. Christ's parables were not just for the people of his time, but also for now.

Hence they must have in their construction a universality which would never become dated. They are simple and deep. In them Jesus gives to people of all ages food for thought and action.

So it can be assumed that those who proclaim the message today can and should transmit the old message in a new form in their own locality, in their own time, in their own way.

Thus the retracing of steps led to defining the role of the Church as that of keeping Christ alive in the minds of each new generation and relating his word to the problems of their time.

In many ways Vatican II seemed to point the Church backward rather than forward. From "teacher of the law" to "teacher of the word."

This may seem like a very simplistic, almost obvious answer to a complicated problem.

And it is. Experience has shown that a positioning exercise is a search for the obvious. Those are the easiest concepts to communicate because they make the most sense to the recipient of a message.

Unfortunately, obvious concepts are also the most difficult to recognize and to sell.

The human mind tends to admire the complicated and dismiss the obvious as being too simplistic. (For example, many clerics in the Catholic Church admire the definition of the role of the Church put forth by a noted theologian named Avery Dulles. His answer: The Church hasn't one role. It has six different roles to play.)

Implementing the position

Once the obvious concept had been isolated, the next thing to be done was to develop the techniques for implementing it.

First and foremost was pulpit training. To fulfill the role of "teacher of the word," the clergy had to become far better speakers and to give far better sermons. (Your best religious speakers today can be found not in church but on Sunday morning television.)

In addition to pulpit training, an introductory film entitled *Return to the Beginning* was proposed.

The start of any major communication effort often needs some drama to get people's attention. The emotion of the film medium is ideal for this kind of effort. (Which is also why television is so powerful a tool for new product introductions.)

A wide range of other program elements was suggested, all carefully constructed around the role of the church as "teacher of the word."

The point here is that once a positioning strategy has been developed, it sets the direction for all the activities of the organization. Even one as large and multifaceted as the Catholic Church.

What happened?

Nothing.

It has been very difficult to convince the management of the Catholic Church to implement this solution to their problems.

Not only do bishops resist having lay people tell them how to run their Church, but the solution appears to be much too obvious for them to accept. Simplicity is not as attractive as complexity.

And as with most big problems, they don't go away. If you've been reading the newspapers, you've probably noted that the Pope is in the process of convening another synod to evaluate the results of Vatican II. The Vatican newspaper *L'Osservatore Romano* said that the synod's purpose was to resolve confusion that has arisen over Vatican II in the 20 years since it ended.

Will they at long last acknowledge the confusion problems? Will they solve their "crisis of identity" and come up with a communications program that repositions the Church in the modern world? Will this program reconcile the widening gulf between liberal and conservative Catholics?

Don't hold your breath.

23

Positioning yourself and your career

If positioning strategies can be used to promote a product, why can't they be used to promote yourself?

No reason at all.

So let's review positioning theory as it might apply to your own personal career.

Define yourself

What are you? People suffer from the same disease as products. They try to be all things to all people.

The problem with this approach is the mind of the prospect. It's difficult enough to link one concept with each product. It's almost impossible with two or three or more concepts.

The most difficult part of positioning is selecting that one specific concept to hang your hat on. Yet you must, if you want to cut through the prospect's wall of indifference.

What are you? What is your own position in life? Can you sum up your own position in a single concept? Then can you run your own career to establish and exploit that position?

Most people aren't ruthless enough to set up a single concept for themselves. They vacillate. They expect others to do it for them.

"I'm the best lawyer in Dallas."

Are you? How often would your name be mentioned if we took a survey of the Dallas legal community?

"I'm the best lawyer in Dallas" is a position that can be achieved with some talent, some luck, and a lot of strategy. And the first step is to isolate the concept that you are going to use to establish that long-term position. It's not easy. But the rewards can be great.

Make mistakes

Anything worthwhile doing is worthwhile doing lousy. If it wasn't worthwhile doing, you shouldn't have done it at all.

On the other hand, if it is worthwhile doing and you wait until you can do it perfectly, if you procrastinate, you run the risk of not doing it. Ever.

Therefore, anything worthwhile doing is worthwhile doing lousy.

Your reputation will probably be better within the company if you try many times and succeed sometimes than if you fear failure and only try for sure things.

People still remember Ty Cobb, who stole 96 bases out of 134 tries (70 percent). But they have forgotton Max Carey, who stole 51 bases out of 53 (96 percent).

Eddie Arcaro, perhaps the greatest jockey who ever rode a horse, had 250 straight losers before he rode his first winner.

Make sure your name is right

Remember Leonard Slye? Few people did, until he changed his name to Roy Rogers, an important first step in becoming a motion picture star.

How about Marion Morrison? A little feminine for a he-man cowboy, so he changed it to John Wayne.

Or Issur Danielovitch? First changed to Isadore Demsky and then to Kirk Douglas.

"Fate tried to conceal him," said Oliver Wendell Holmes, Jr., "by naming him Smith."

Common law grants you the right to adopt any name you want as long as you're not trying to defraud or be deceptive. So don't change your name to McDonald and open up a hamburger stand.

Also, if you're a politician, don't bother to change your name to "None of the Above." Luther D. Knox, a candidate in a Louisiana gubernatorial primary, had his name legally changed to just that. However, a federal judge had Mr. None of the Above's name taken off the ballot because the move was deceptive.

Avoid the no-name trap

Many business people fall victim to initialitus personally as well as corporately.

As young executives, they notice that top managers usually use initials: J. S. Smith, R. H. Jones. So they do the same. On memos and in letters.

It's a mistake. You can afford to do that only if everyone knows who you are. If you're on your way up, if you're trying to burn your name into the minds of top management, you need a name, not a set of initials. For exactly the same reasons your company does.

Write your name and look at it. Roger P. Dinkelacker.

What a name like this says psychologically to management is: We are such a big company and you have such an insignificant job that you must use the "P" to differentiate yourself from the other Roger Dinkelackers on the staff.

Not likely.

It is possible, if your name is something like John Smith or Mary Jones, that you actually do need a middle initial to differentiate yourself from the other John Smiths or Mary Joneses.

If so, what you really need is a new name. Confusion is the enemy of successful positioning. You can't "burn in" a name that's too common. How are other people going to differentiate between John T. Smith and John S. Smith?

They won't bother. They'll just forget you along with the rest. And the no-name trap will have claimed another victim.

Avoid the line-extension trap

If you had three daughters, would you name them Mary 1, Mary 2, and Mary 3? As a matter of fact, would you name them Mary, Marian, and Marilyn? Either way, you're creating a lifetime of confusion.

When you hang a junior on your son's name, you do him no favor. He deserves a separate identity.

In show business, where you must burn a clearcut identity in the mind of the public, even a famous last name should probably not be used.

Today Liza Minnelli is a bigger star than her mother, Judy Garland, ever was. As Liza Garland, she would have started with a handicap.

Frank Sinatra, Jr., is an example of the most difficult kind of line-extension name. He literally started with two strikes against him.

With a name like Frank Sinatra, Jr., the audience says to itself, "He's not going to be able to sing as well as his father."

Since you hear what you expect to hear, of course he doesn't.

Find a horse to ride

Some ambitious, intelligent people find themselves trapped in situations where their future looks bleak. So what do they generally do?

They try harder. They try to compensate by long hours of hard work and effort. The secret of success is to keep your nose to the grindstone, do your job better than the next person, and fame and fortune will come your way, right?

Wrong. Trying harder is rarely the pathway to success. Trying smarter is the better way.

It's the story of the shoemaker's children all over again. Too often, management people don't know how to manage their own careers.

Their own promotional strategy is often based on the naive assumption that ability and hard work are all that counts. And so they dig in and work harder, waiting for the day that someone will tap them on the shoulder with the magic wand.

But that day seldom comes.

The truth is, the road to fame and fortune is rarely found within yourself. The only sure way to success is to find yourself a horse to ride. It may be difficult for the ego to accept, but success in life is based more on what others can do for you than on what you can do for yourself.

Kennedy was wrong. Ask not what you can do for your company. Ask what your company can do for you. Therefore, if you want to take maximum advantage of the opportunities that your career has to offer, you must keep your eyes open and find yourself a horse to do the job for you.

The first horse to ride is your company. Where is your company going? Or more impolitely, is it going anywhere at all?

Too many good people have taken their good prospects and locked them into situations that are doomed to failure. But failure at least gives you a second chance. Even worse is the company with less than average chances for growth.

No matter how brilliant you are, it never pays to cast your lot with a loser. Even the best officer on the Titanic wound up in the same lifeboat as the worst. And that's if he was lucky enough to stay out of the water.

You can't do it yourself. If your company is going nowhere, get yourself a new one. While you can't always pick an IBM or a Xerox, you ought to be able to do considerably better than average.

Place your bets on the growth industries. Tomorrow-type products like computers, electronics, optics, communications.

And don't forget that soft services of all types are growing at a much faster rate than hard products. So look at banks, leasing, insurance, medical, financial, and consulting service companies.

Don't forget that your experience with yesterday-type products can blind you to opportunities in totally different product areas. And especially services.

And when you change jobs to join one of those tomorrow-type companies, don't just ask how much they are going to pay you today.

Also ask how much they are likely to pay you tomorrow.

The second horse to ride is your boss. Ask yourself the same questions about your boss as you asked yourself about your company.

Is he or she going anywhere? If not, who is? Always try to work for the smartest, brightest, most competent person you can find.

If you look at biographies of successful people, it's amazing to find how many crawled up the ladder of success right behind someone else. From their first assignment in some menial job to their last as president or CEO of a major company.

Yet some people actually like to work for incompetents. I suppose they feel that a fresh flower stands out better if it's surrounded by wilted ones. They forget the tendency of top management to throw the whole bunch out if they become dissatisfied with an operation.

Two types of individuals come in looking for jobs.

One is inordinately proud of his or her specialty. He or she will often say, "You people really need me around here. You're weak in my specialty."

The other type says just the opposite. "You're strong in my specialty. You do a terrific job, and I want to work with the best."

Which type is more likely to get the job? Right. The latter person.

On the other hand, strange as it might seem, top management people see more of the other type. The person who wants to be an expert. Preferably with a big title and salary to match.

"Hitch your wagon to a star," said Ralph Waldo Emerson. Good advice then. Even better advice now.

If your boss is going places, chances are good that you are too.

The third horse to ride is a friend.   Many business people have an enormous number of personal friends but no business friends. And while personal friends are awfully nice to have and can sometimes get you a deal on a TV set or braces for the kids, they're usually not too helpful when it comes to finding a better job.

Most of the big breaks that happen in a person's career happen because a business friend recommended that person.

The more business friends you make outside of your own organization, the more likely you are to wind up in a big, rewarding job.

It's not enough just to make friends. You have to take out that friendship horse and exercise it once in a while. If you don't you won't be able to ride it when you need it.

When an old business friend you haven't heard from in 10 years calls you and wants to have lunch, you know two things will happen: (1) you're going to pay for the lunch, and (2) your friend is looking for a job.

When you need a job, it's usually too late to try that type of tactic. The way to ride the friendship horse is to keep in touch regularly with all your business friends.

Send them tear sheets of articles they may be interested in, clips of publicity items, and congratulatory letters when they get promoted.

And don't assume people always see stories that might have mentioned them. They don't. And they always appreciate it when someone sends them an item they may have missed.

The fourth horse to ride is an idea.   On the night before he died, Victor Hugo wrote in his diary, "Nothing, not all the armies of the world, can stop an idea whose time has come."

Everyone knows that an idea can take you to the top faster than anything else. But people sometimes expect too much of an idea. They want one that is not only great, but one that everyone else thinks is great too.

There are no such ideas. If you wait until an idea is ready to be accepted, it's too late. Someone else will have preempted it.

Or in the in-out vocabulary of a few years ago: Anything definitely in is already on its way out.

To ride the "idea" horse, you must be willing to expose yourself to ridicule and controversy. You must be willing to go against the tide.

You can't be first with a new idea or concept unless you are willing to stick your neck out. And take a lot of abuse. And bide your time until your time comes.

"One indication of the validity of a principle," according to psychologist Charles Osgood, "is the vigor and persistence with which it is opposed." "In any field," says Dr. Osgood, "if people see that a principle is obvious nonsense and easy to refute, they tend to ignore it. On the other hand, if the principle is difficult to refute and it causes them to question some of their own basic assumptions with which their names may be identified, they have to go out of their way to find something wrong with it."

Never be afraid of conflict.

Where would Winston Churchill have been without Adolf Hitler? We know the answer to that one. After Adolf Hitler was disposed of, at the very first opportunity the British public promptly turned Winston Churchill out of office.

And you remember what Liberace said about the bad reviews one of his concerts received. "I cried all the way to the bank."

An idea or concept without an element of conflict is not an idea at all. It's motherhood, apple pie, and the flag, revisited.

The fifth horse to ride is faith.   Faith in others and their ideas. The importance of getting outside of yourself, of finding your fortune on the outside, is illustrated by the story of a man who was a failure most of his life.

His name was Ray Kroc, and he was a lot older than most

people and a failure to boot when he met two brothers who changed his life.

For the brothers had an idea, but no faith. So they sold their idea as well as their name to Ray Kroc for relatively few dollars.

Ray Kroc became one of the richest people in America. Worth hundreds of millions of dollars.

The brothers? They were the McDonald brothers, and every time you eat one of their hamburgers, remember it was the vision, courage, and persistence of the outsider who made the McDonald's chain a success. Not two guys named McDonald.

The sixth horse to ride is yourself.   There is one other horse. An animal that is mean, difficult, and unpredictable. Yet people often try to ride it. With very little success.

That horse is yourself. It is possible to succeed in business or in life all by yourself. But it's not easy.

Like life itself, business is a social activity. As much cooperation as competition.

Take selling, for example, You don't make a sale all by yourself. Somebody also has to buy what you're selling.

So remember, the winningest jockeys are not necessarily the lightest, the smartest, or the strongest. The best jockey doesn't win the race.

The jockey that wins the race is usually the one with the best horse.

So pick yourself a horse to ride and then ride it for all it's worth.

24

Positioning your business

How do you get started on a positioning program?

It's not easy. The temptation is to work on the solution without first thinking through the problem. Much better to think about your situation in an organized way before leaping to a conclusion.

To help you with this thinking process, here are six questions you can ask yourself to get your mental juices flowing.

Don't be deceived. The questions are simple to ask but difficult to answer. They often raise soul-searching issues that can test your courage and your beliefs.

1. What position do you own?

Positioning is thinking in reverse. Instead of starting with yourself, you start with the mind of the prospect.

Instead of asking what you are, you ask what position you already own in the mind of the prospect.

Changing minds in our overcommunicated society is an extremely difficult task. It's much easier to work with what's already there.

In determining the state of the prospect's mind, it's important not to let corporate egos get in the way. You get the answer to the question "What position do we own?" from the market-place, not from the marketing manager.

If this requires a few dollars for research, so be it. Spend the money. It's better to know exactly what you're up against now than to discover it later when nothing can be done about it.

Don't be narrow-minded. You must look at the big picture, not the details.

Sabena's problem is not Sabena, the airline, but Belgium, the country.

Seven-Up's problem is not the prospect's attitude toward lemon/lime drinks, but the overwhelming share of mind occupied by the colas. "Get me a soda," to many people, means a Coke or a Pepsi.

Looking at the big picture helped Seven-Up develop its successful uncola program.

Most products today are like 7-Up before the uncola campaign. They have weak or nonexistent positions in the minds of most prospects.

What you must do is to find a way into the mind by hooking your product, service, or concept to what's already there.

2. What position do you want to own?

Here is where you bring out your crystal ball and try to figure out the best position to own from a long-term point of view. "Own" is the key word. Too many programs set out to communicate a position that is impossible to preempt because someone else already owns it.

Ford failed to position the Edsel successfully. One reason was there simply was no room in the mind of the auto buyer for another heavily chromed, medium-priced car.

On the other hand, when Richardson Merrill was trying to position an entry in the cold-remedy field against Contac and Dristan, it wisely avoided a direct confrontation. Leaving these two to fight it out in the daylight hours, Richardson Merrill chose to preempt the "nightmare cold remedy" position for Nyquil.

Nyquil turned out to be the most successful new product they have introduced in recent years.

Sometimes you can want too much. You can want to own a position that's too broad. A position that can't be established in the prospect's mind. And even if it could, it couldn't be defended against the assaults of narrowly based products like Nyquil.

This, of course, is the everybody trap, and one example is a famous campaign for a beer called Rheingold. This brewery wanted to preempt New York City's working class. (Not a bad objective when you consider the large number of heavy beer drinkers in this group.)

So they produced some marvelous commercials featuring Italians drinking Rheingold, Blacks drinking Rheingold, Irish drinking Rheingold, Jews drinking Rheingold, and so on.

Well, rather than appeal to everybody, they ended up appealing to nobody. The reason was simple. Prejudice being a basic human commodity, the fact that one ethnic group drank Rheingold sure didn't impress another ethnic group.

In fact, all the campaign did was alienate every ethnic group in New York.

In your own career, it's easy to make the same mistake. If you try to be all things to all people, you wind up with nothing. Better to narrow the focus of your expertise. To establish a unique position as a specialist, not as a jack-of-all-trades generalist.

The job market today belongs to the people who can define and position themselves as specialists.

3. Whom must you outgun?

If your proposed position calls for a head-to-head approach against a marketing leader, forget it. It's better to go around an obstacle rather than over it. Back up. Try to select a position that no one else has a firm grip on.

You must spend as much time thinking about the situation from the point of view of your competitors as you do thinking about it from your own.

Prospects don't buy, they choose. Among brands of automobiles. Among brands of beer. Among brands of computers. The merit, or lack of merit, of your brand is not nearly as important as your position among the possible choices.

Often to create a viable position, you must reposition another brand or even an entire category of product. As Tylenol did to aspirin, for example.

Notice what happens when you fail to deal with the competition. Bristol-Myers spent $35 million to launch Nuprin, and American Home Products spent $40 million to launch Advil. Both products contain ibuprofen, an analgesic new to America.

But both campaigns failed to reposition Tylenol, the dominant headache remedy on the market. As a result, neither product has been able to carve out more than a tiny market share.

Coming to grips with the competition is the main problem in most marketing situations.

4. Do you have enough money?

A big obstacle to successful positioning is attempting to achieve the impossible. It takes money to build a share of mind. It takes money to establish a position. It takes money to hold a position once you've established it.

The noise level today is fierce. There are just too many me-too products and too many me-too companies vying for the mind of the prospect. Getting noticed is getting tougher.

During the course of a single year, the average human mind is exposed to some 200,000 advertising messages. When you remember that a 30-second $500,000 Super Bowl commercial can make only one of those 200,000 impressions, the odds against an advertiser today must be seen as enormous.

This is why a company like Procter & Gamble is such a formidable competitor. When it bets on a new product, it will slide

$50 million on the table, look around at the competition, and say, "Your bet."

If you don't spend enough to get above the noise level, you allow the Procter & Gambles of this world to take your concept away from you. One way to cope with the noise-level problem is to reduce the geographic scope of your problem. To introduce new products or new ideas on a market-by-market basis rather than nationally or even internationally.

With a given number of dollars, it's better to overspend in one city than to underspend in several cities. If you become successful in one location, you can always roll out the program to other places. Provided the first location is appropriate.

If you can become the No. 1 scotch in New York (the No. 1 scotch-drinking area of the country), you can roll out the product to the rest of the U.S.A.

5. Can you stick it out?

You can think of our overcommunicated society as a constant crucible of change. As one idea replaces another in bewildering succession.

To cope with change, it's important to take a long-range point of view. To determine your basic position and then stick to it.

Positioning is a concept that is cumulative. Something that takes advantage of advertising's long-range nature.

You have to hang in there, year after year. Most successful companies rarely change a winning formula. How many years have you seen those Marlboro men riding into the sunset? Crest has been fighting cavities for so long they're into their second generation of kids. Because of change, a company must think even more strategically than it did before.

With rare exceptions, a company should almost never change its basic positioning strategy. Only its tactics, those short-term maneuvers that are intended to implement a long-term strategy.

The trick is to take that basic strategy and improve it. Find new ways to dramatize it. New ways to avoid the boredom factor. In other words, new ways to have Ronald McDonald end up eating a hamburger.

Owning a position in the mind is like owning a valuable piece of real estate. Once you give it up, you might find it's impossible to get it back again.

The line-extension trap is a good example. What you are really doing when you line-extend is weakening your basic position. And once that's gone, you are adrift without an anchor.

Levi's line-extended into casual clothes. And then found its basic position in jeans undermined by "designer label" jeans.

6. Do you match your position?

Creative people often resist positioning thinking because they believe it restricts their creativity.

And you know what? It does. Positioning thinking does restrict creativity.

One of the great communication tragedies is to watch an organization go through a careful planning exercise, step by step, complete with charts and graphs and then turn the strategy over to the "creatives" for execution. They, in turn, apply their skills and the strategy disappears in a cloud of technique, never to be recognized again.

An institution like this would have been much better off running the flip-chart with the strategy on it rather than the ad with thousands of dollars worth of creativity applied.

"Avis is only No. 2 in rent-a-cars, so why go with us? We try harder." This doesn't sound like an ad. It sounds like the presentation of the marketing strategy. In truth, it's both.

Do your advertisements for yourself match your position? Do your clothes, for example, tell the world that you're a banker or a lawyer or an artist?

Or do you wear creative clothes that undermine your position?

Creativity by itself is worthless. Only when it is subordinated to the positioning objective can creativity make a contribution.

The role of the outsider

The question sometimes arises: Do we do it ourselves or do we hire someone to position us?

The someone that often gets hired is an advertising agency. An ad agency? Who needs help from those Madison Avenue hucksters?

Everybody. But only the rich can afford to hire an advertising agency. All the others have to learn how to do it themselves. Have to learn how to apply the invaluable ingredient only available from the outsider.

And what does the outsider supply? An ingredient called ignorance. In other words, objectivity.

By not knowing what goes on inside a company, the outsider is better able to see what is happening on the outside. In the mind of the prospect.

The outsider is naturally attuned to outside-in thinking, while the insider is more comfortable with inside-out thinking.

Objectivity is the key ingredient supplied by the advertising or marketing communication or public relations agency.

What the outsider doesn't supply

In a word, magic. Some business managers believe that the role of an advertising agency is to wave a magic wand which causes prospects to immediately rush out and buy the product.

The wand, of course, is called "creativity," a commodity much sought after by the neophyte advertiser.

The popular view is that the agency "creates." And that the best agencies are filled with a substance called "creativity" which they liberally apply to their advertising solutions.

In advertising circles, the story is told about an advertising agency that was very creative. So creative, in fact, it could take straw and spin it into gold.

Now you might have heard of them because they had a very creative name. Rumplestiltskin, Inc.

The legend lives on. Even today, some people think agencies are so creative that they can spin straw into gold.

Not true. Advertising agencies can't spin straw into gold. If they could, they'd be in the straw-spinning business and not the advertising business.

Today, creativity is dead. The name of the game on Madison Avenue is positioning.

25

Playing the positioning game

Some people have trouble playing the positioning game because they are hung up on words.

They assume, incorrectly, that words have meanings. They let Mr. Webster rule their life.

You must understand the role of words

As general semanticists have been saying for decades, words don't contain meanings. The meanings are not in the words. They are in the people using the words.

Like a sugar bowl which is empty until someone fills it with sugar, a word has no meaning until someone uses it and fills it with meaning.

If you try to add sugar to a leaky sugar bowl, you won't get anywhere. So, too, if you try to add meaning to a leaky word. Much better to discard that leaky word and use another.

The word "Volkswagen" won't hold the concept of a medium-sized luxury car, so you discard that sugar bowl and use another, "Audi," which holds the concept better. You don't insist that because it's made in a Volkswagen factory, it must be a Volkswagen. Mental rigidity is a barrier to successful positioning.

(While Volkswagen faltered in the American market, Audi boomed. Currently Audi outsells BMW and is breathing down the neck of Mercedes-Benz.)

To be successful today at positioning, you must have a large degree of mental flexibility. You must be able to select and use words with as much disdain for the history book as for the dictionary.

Not that conventional, accepted meanings are not important. Quite the contrary. You must select the words which trigger the meanings you want to establish.

But is this ethical? Remember, words have no meaning. They are empty containers until you fill them with meaning. If you want to reposition a product, a person, or a country, you often have to first change the container.

In a sense, every product or service is "packaged goods." If it isn't sold in a box, the name becomes the box.

You must know how words affect people

Words are triggers. They trigger the meanings which are buried in the mind.

Of course, if people understood this, there would be no advantage in renaming a product or selecting emotional words like Mustang for an automobile.

But they don't. Most people are "unsane." They're not completely sane and they're not completely insane. They're somewhere in between.

What's the difference between sane people and insane people? What exactly do insane people do? Alfred Korzybski, who developed the concept of general semantics, explains that insane people try to make the world of reality fit what is in their heads.

The insane person who thinks he is Napoleon makes the outside world fit that notion.

The sane person constantly analyzes the world of reality and then changes what's inside his or her head to fit the facts.

That's an awful lot of trouble for most people. Besides, how many people want to constantly change their opinions to fit the facts?

It's a whole lot easier to change the facts to fit your opinions.

Unsane people make up their minds and then find the facts to "verify" their opinion. Or even more commonly, they accept the opinion of the nearest "expert," and then they don't have to bother with the facts at all.

So you see the power of the psychologically right name. The mind makes the world of reality fit the name. A Mustang looks sportier, racier, and faster than if the same car had been called the Turtle.

Language is the currency of the mind. To think conceptually, you manipulate words. With the right choice of words, you can influence the thinking process itself. (As proof that the mind "thinks with words" and not abstract thoughts, consider how a language is learned. To be really fluent in a foreign language, say French, you must learn to think in French.)

But there are limits. If a word is so far out of touch with reality, the mind just refuses to use the word. It says "large" on the tube that everyone except the manufacturer calls a "small" toothpaste tube. It says "economy" on the tube that everyone calls "large."

The People's Republic of China is usually called "Red China" because no one believes it is a "people's republic." (Inside the country, the People's Republic of China is undoubtedly an effective name.)

You must be careful of change

The more things change, the more they remain the same. Yet people today are caught up in the illusion of change. Every day, the world seems to be turning faster.

Years ago a successful product might live 50 years or more before fading away. Today a product's life cycle is much shorter. Sometimes it can be measured in months instead of years.

New products, new services, new markets, even new media are constantly being born. They grow to adulthood and then slide to oblivion. And a new cycle starts again.

Yesterday the way to reach the masses was the mass magazines. Today it's network TV. Tomorrow it could be cable. The only permanent thing today seems to be change. The kaleidoscope of life clicks faster and faster. New patterns emerge and disappear.

Change has become a way of life for many companies. But is change the way to keep pace with change? The exact opposite appears to be true.

The landscape is littered with the debris of projects that companies rushed into in attempting to keep pace. Singer trying to move into the boom in home appliances. RCA moving into the boom in computers. General Foods moving into the boom in fast-food outlets. Not to mention the hundreds of companies that threw away their corporate identities to chase the passing fad to initials.

Meanwhile the programs of those who kept at what they did best and held their ground have been immensely successful. Maytag selling its reliable appliances. Walt Disney selling the world of fantasy and fun. Avon calling.

You need vision

Change is a wave on the ocean of time. Short-term, the waves cause agitation and confusion. Long-term, the underlying currents are much more significant. To cope with change, you have to take a long-range point of view. To determine your basic business and stick with it.

Changing the direction of a large company is like trying to turn an aircraft carrier. It takes a mile before anything happens. And if it was a wrong turn, getting back on course takes even longer.

To play the game successfully, you must make decisions on what your company will be doing not next month or next year but in 5 years, 10 years. In other words, instead of turning the wheel to meet each fresh wave, a company must point itself in the right direction.

You must have vision. There's no sense building a position based on a technology that's too narrow. Or a product that's becoming obsolete. Or a name that's defective.

Most of all, you have to be able to see the difference between what works and what doesn't work.

Sounds simple, but it's not. When the tide is rising, everything seems to be working. When the tide is falling, nothing seems to be working.

You have to learn how to separate your efforts from the general movement of the economy. Many marketing experts are blessed with a generous supply of luck. Be wary. Today's hula-hoop marketing genius could be tomorrow's welfare recipient.

Be patient. The sun shines tomorrow on those who have made the right decisions today.

If a company has positioned itself in the right direction, it will be able to ride the currents of change, ready to take advantage of those opportunities that are right for it. But when an opportunity arrives, a company must move quickly.

You need courage

When you trace the history of how leadership positions were established, from Hershey in chocolate to Hertz in rent-a-cars, the common thread is not marketing skill or even product innovation. The common thread is seizing the initiative before the competitor has a chance to get established. The leader usually poured in the marketing money while the situation was still fluid.

Hershey, for example, established a position in chocolate so strong that Hershey felt it didn't need to advertise at all. This conviction was a luxury that competitors like Mars couldn't afford.

Finally Hershey decided to advertise. But not in time. Today the Hershey milk chocolate bar is not the largest seller. It's not even in the top 5.

You can see that establishing a leadership position depends not only on luck and timing but also on a willingness to pour it on when others stand back and wait.

You need objectivity

To be successful in the positioning era, you must be brutally frank. You must try to eliminate all ego from the decision-making process. It only clouds the issue.

One of the most critical aspects of positioning is being able to evaluate products objectively and see how they are viewed by customers and prospects.

You also have to remember that you can't play basketball without a backboard. You need someone to bounce your ideas off. As soon as you think you have found that simple idea that is the solution to your problem, you have lost something.

You have lost your objectivity. You need the other person to take a fresh look at what you have wrought. And vice versa.

Like Ping-Pong, positioning is a game best played by two people. It's no accident that this book was written by two people. Only in a give-and-take atmosphere can ideas be refined and perfected.

You need simplicity

Only an obvious idea will work today. The overwhelming volume of communication prevents anything else from succeeding.

But the obvious isn't always so obvious. "Boss" Kettering had a sign which he placed on the wall of the General Motors Research Building in Dayton: "This problem when solved will be simple."

"Raisins from California. Nature's candy."

"Moist and meaty Gainesburgers. The canned dog food without the can."

"Bubble Yum. Number yum in bubble gum."

These are the kinds of simple ideas that work today. Simple concepts expressed with simple words used in a straightforward way.

Often the solution to a problem is so simple that thousands of people have looked at it without seeing it. When an idea is clever or complicated, however, we should be suspicious. It probably won't work because it's not simple enough.

The history of science is a history of the Ketterings of this world who found simple solutions to complex problems.

The head of an advertising agency once insisted that his account executives paste down the marketing strategy on the back of each layout.

Then when the client asked what the ad was supposed to do, the account person could turn the layout over and read the strategy.

But an ad should be simple enough so that it is the strategy.

The agency made a mistake. It ran the wrong side of the layout.

You need subtlety

Beginners who play the positioning game often remark, "How easy this is. You just find a position you can call your own."

Simple, yes. But easy, no.

The difficulty is finding an open position that's also effective. In politics, for example, it's easy to establish a position to the far right (a conservative position) or the far left (a socialist position). You will undoubtedly preempt either position.

You will also lose.

What you must do is to find an opening near the center of the spectrum. You must be slightly conservative in a field of liberals or slightly liberal in a field of conservatives.

This calls for great restraint and subtlety. The big winners in business and in life are those people who have found open positions near the center of the spectrum. Not at the edge.

You can sometimes have a positioning success and a sales failure. This might be termed "Rolls-Royce thinking."

"We're the Rolls-Royce of the industry" is a claim you often hear in business today.

Do you know how many Rolls-Royces are sold in America every year?

About a thousand, or 0.01 percent of the market. Cadillac, on the other hand, sells more than 300,000.

Both Cadillac and Rolls-Royce are luxury cars, but the gulf between them is enormous. To the average automobile buyer, the Rolls-Royce at $100,000 and up is out of reach.

Cadillac, like Michelob and other premium products, is not. The secret to establishing a successful position is to keep two things in balance: (1) A unique position with (2) an appeal that's not too narrow.

You must be willing to sacrifice

The essence of positioning is sacrifice. You must be willing to give up something in order to establish that unique position.

Nyquil, the nighttime cold medicine, gave up the daytime market.

The focus of most marketing operations is just the opposite. They look for ways to broaden their markets by line extension, by size and flavor proliferation, by multiple distribution. All these things tend to produce short-term sales increases and long-term positioning erosion.

In positioning, smaller may be better. It is usually better to look for smaller targets that you can own exclusively rather than a bigger market you have to share with three or four other brands.

You can't be all things to all people and still have a powerful position.

You need patience

Very few companies can afford to launch a new product on a nationwide scale.

Instead they look for places to make the brand successful. And then roll it out to other markets.

The geographic roll-out is one way. You build the product in one market and then move on to another. From east to west. Or vice versa.

The demographic roll-out is another. Philip Morris built Marlboro into the No. 1 cigarette on college campuses long before it became the No. 1 brand nationwide.

The chronologic roll-out is the third way. You build the brand among a specific age group and then roll it out to others. "The Pepsi Generation" helped Pepsi-Cola build the product among the younger set and then reap the benefits as they grew up.

Distribution is another roll-out technique. The Wella line was first sold through beauty salons. After the products were established, they were sold through drugstores and supermarkets.

You need a global outlook

Don't overlook the importance of worldwide thinking. A company that keeps its eye on Tom, Dick, and Harry is going to miss Pierre, Hans, and Yoshio.

Marketing is rapidly becoming a worldwide ballgame. A company that owns a position in one country now finds that it can use that position to wedge its way into another. IBM has some 60 percent of the German computer market. Is this fact surprising? It shouldn't be. IBM earns more than 50 percent of its profits outside the United States.

As companies start to operate on a worldwide basis, they often discover they have a name problem.

A typical example is U.S. Rubber, a worldwide company that marketed many products not made of rubber. Changing the name to Uniroyal created a new corporate identity that could be used worldwide.

What you don't need

You don't need a reputation as a marketing genius. As a matter of fact, this could be a fatal flaw.

All too often, the product leader makes the fatal mistake of attributing its success to marketing skill. As a result, it thinks it can transfer that skill to other products and other marketing situations.

Witness, for example, the disappointing record of Xerox in computers.

And the mecca of marketing knowledge, International Business Machines Corporation, hasn't done much better. So far, IBM's plain-paper copier hasn't made much of a dent in Xerox's business. Touché.

The rules of positioning hold for all types of products. In the packaged-goods area, for example, Bristol-Myers tried to take on Crest toothpaste with Fact (killed after $5 million was spent on promotion). Then they tried to go after Alka-Seltzer with Resolve (killed after $11 million was spent). Then they tried to unseat Bayer with Dissolve, another financial headache.

The suicidal bent of companies that go head-on against established competition is hard to understand.

Hope springs eternal in the human breast. Nine times out of ten, the also-ran that sets out to attack the leader head-on is headed for disaster.

To repeat, the first rule of positioning is: To win the battle for the mind, you can't compete head-on against a company that has a strong, established position. You can go around, under or over, but never head to head.

The leader owns the high ground. The No. 1 position in the prospect's mind. The top rung of the product ladder. To move up the ladder, you must follow the rules of positioning.

In our overcommunicated society, the name of the game today is positioning.

And only the better players are going to survive.

Index

Advertising:
  comparative, 32–34, 66
  image era of, 24
  and the marketplace of today,
    22–23
  positioning era of, 24–27
  product era of, 23–24
Advertising explosion, 17–18
Age and positioning strategy, 58
Airlines, 79–80, 93, 137–138
Anonymity, 99–100
Automobile rental, 3, 33–35, 198,
  205
Automobiles, 14, 31, 45, 47, 54–56,
  58–59, 120–123, 128–129,
  201–202

Banks, 159–171
Batteries, 103–104, 108
Beer, 25–27, 30, 55, 57, 58, 72, 195
Belgium, 137–142
"Broadening the base," 112–113

"Can do" spirit, 37–40
Candy, 149–152, 205–206
Cars (see Automobile rental; Auto-
  mobiles)
Catholic Church, 177–182
Change, effect of, on positioning,
  203–204
Chewing gum, 107–108
China (dinnerware), 63
Cigarettes, 57, 109–110
Coffee, 3, 111
Cold remedies, 58, 194–195
Communication, 6
  excessive volume of, 11–13
  media explosion, 15–16
  oversimplified message, 7–9

Comparative advertising, 3, 32–34,
  66, 68
Computers, 24, 38–42, 46, 98, 131–
  134
Conglomerates, 95–96
Copiers, 44, 47–49, 99, 131–134
Corporate names (see Names, cor-
  porate)
Creneaus, 54–61

Detergents, 49–50, 97
Distribution as positioning strategy,
  58
Diversification, 130–131

Ethics, 67–69
Everybody trap, 60

Free-ride trap, 95–100
F.W.M.T.S. trap, 34–35

Generic names, 102–103
Given names, 77–78

Hand lotion, 111–112
House names, 124–125
Human mind (see Mind)

Inside-out thinking, 101–102, 199

Jamaica, 143–147
Jewelry, 56

Leaders, market (see Market leaders)
Line extension:
  advantages of, 115–116

Line extension (*Cont.*):
  bartender test for, 119–120
  disadvantages of, 116–118
  examples of, 103–112
  and inside-out thinking, 101–102,
    199
  list test for, 118–119
  and outside-in thinking, 102–103,
    199
  and personal names, 186
  reverse, 112–113
  rules for, 124–125
Line-extension trap, 101–113, 186
Long Island Trust Company, 159–
  165

Mailgram, 153–158
Margarine, 110–111
Market leaders:
  actions to be avoided, 46
  effect of name change on, 50–51
  establishing position, 43
  failures of, 44
  maintaining position, 45–46
  and multibrand strategy, 49–50
  and power of the product, 48–49
  protecting against the unexpect-
    ed, 47–48
  reinforcing position, 47
  and temporary equality, 45
Media explosion, 15–16
Milk Duds, 149–152
Mind:
  capacity of, 30–31
  easy way into, 19–21
  hard way into, 21–22
  mapping of the prospect's, 160–
    163
  oversimplified, 6–7
  response of, to expectations, 29–
    30
Mouthwash, 65–66

Names:
  corporate, 78–80, 128–129

Names (*Cont.*):
  and acronyms, 93
  and conglomerates, 95–96
  house, 124–125
  obsolescence of, 90–92
  and phonetics, 85–86
  reason for selection errors, 89–
    90
  shortened to initials, 86–91, 94
  similarity of, 80–83
  and telephone directories, 94
  generic, 102–103
  given, 77–78
  personal, 184–186
  product: choosing, 71–74, 96–
    100
    coined, 74–75
    compared to rubber bands,
      123–124
    negative, 75–77
No-name trap, 85–94, 185–186

Outside-in thinking, 102–103, 199
Overcommunicated society, 6
Oversimplified message, 7–9
Oversimplified mind, 6–7

Pain relievers, 62–63, 95, 102, 105,
  196
Paper products, 106–107
Perfume, 55, 58
Personal names, 184–186
Politicians, 8, 13–14, 37, 62, 65, 78,
  86–87, 100
Positioning, 5
  against undisputed leader, 40–42
  for a business, 193–200
  defined, 2–3
  effect of change on, 203–204
  major examples of: banks, 159–
    165, 167–171
    a church, 177–182
    a company, 127–136
    a country, 137–142

Positioning, major examples of
        (*Cont.*):
    an island, 143–147
    a product, 149–152
    a service, 153–158
    a ski resort, 173–175
    yourself and your career, 183–
        191
    origin of, 3–4
    personal characteristics for: cour-
        age, 205–206
        global outlook, 209–210
        objectivity, 206
        patience, 209
        sacrifice, 208
        simplicity, 206–207
        subtlety, 207–208
        vision, 204–205
    rules for, 201–210
Positioning strategies:
    age, 58
    appealing to everyone, 60
    comparative advertising, 32–34,
        66
    distribution, 58
    and existing product line, 58–59
    heavy usage, 58
    high price, 55–56
    low price, 56–57
    sex, 57–58
    size, 54–55
    and technology, 59–60
    time of day, 58
    unique, 34
Potato chips, 64–65
Price as positioning strategy, 55–57
Product explosion, 16–17, 32
Product failure, reasons for, 53–54
Product names (*see* Names, prod-
    uct)

Repositioning:
    changing existing attitudes, 61–
        62
    and comparative advertising, 66

Repositioning (*Cont.*):
    and ethics, 67–69
    examples of, 62–66
    legality of, 67
Reverse line extension, 112–113

Semantic differential research, 160
"Sensory overload," 17
Sex as positioning strategy, 57–58
Shampoo, 105–106, 112–113
Size as positioning strategy, 54–55
Soft drinks, 3, 34, 44, 47–49, 74,
    104–105, 194
Stowe ski resort, 173–175

Technology as positioning strategy,
    59–60, 134–136
Technology trap, 59–60
Toothpaste, 58, 66
Tourism, 137–147, 173–175
Traps:
    everybody, 60
    free-ride, 95–100
    F.W.M.T.S., 34–35
    line-extension, 101–113, 186
    no-name, 85–94, 185–186
    technology, 59–60

United Jersey Bank, 167–171

Vodka, 60, 63–64

Whisky, 59–60, 110, 119–120
Words:
    effect of, on people, 202–203
    role of, in positioning, 201–202

Xerox Corporation, 24, 42, 44, 47–
    50, 97–99, 127–136